ArtScroll Series®

Rabbi Nosson Scherman / Rabbi Meir Zlotowitz

General Editors

The Zeide

Published by
Mesorah Publications, ltd

RABBI ABRAHAM J. TWERSKI, M.D.

Reb
Motele

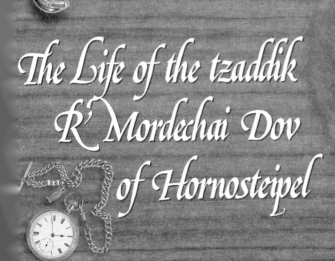

*The Life of the tzaddik
R' Mordechai Dov
of Hornosteipel*

FIRST EDITION
First Impression … November 2002

Published and Distributed by
MESORAH PUBLICATIONS, LTD.
4401 Second Avenue / Brooklyn, N.Y 11232

Distributed in Europe by
LEHMANNS
Unit E, Viking Industrial Park
Rolling Mill Road
Jarow, Tyne & Wear, NE32 3DP
England

Distributed in Australia and New Zealand by
GOLDS WORLD OF JUDAICA
3-13 William Street
Balaclava, Melbourne 3183
Victoria, Australia

Distributed in Israel by
SIFRIATI / A. GITLER — BOOKS
6 Hayarkon Street
Bnei Brak 51127

Distributed in South Africa by
KOLLEL BOOKSHOP
Shop 8A Norwood Hypermarket
Norwood 2196, Johannesburg, South Africa

ARTSCROLL SERIES®
THE ZEIDE REB MOTELE
© Copyright 2002, by MESORAH PUBLICATIONS, Ltd.
4401 Second Avenue / Brooklyn, N.Y. 11232 / (718) 921-9000 / www.artscroll.com

Typography by CompuScribe at ArtScroll Studios, Ltd.

Printed in the United States of America by Noble Book Press Corp.
Bound by Sefercraft, Quality Bookbinders, Ltd., Brooklyn N.Y. 11232

Dedicated to all the descendants of

Zeide R' Motele,

whose legacy endows them
with much pride and with an
awesome responsibility.

Table of Contents

Introduction

I was taught that *yichus* (genealogy) can be both an asset and a liability. It is an asset in that it can give a person a sense of pride and worthiness. The great interest in searching for one's roots attests to this. It is a liability in that when one compares oneself to one's forebears, one's self-esteem may shrink to microscopic size.

The latter thought is contained in the commentary of the *Shelah* on the verse: "I will remember My covenant with Jacob and also My covenant with Isaac, and also My covenant with Abraham will I remember" (*Leviticus* 26:42). Elsewhere in the Torah, the Patriarchs are always mentioned in a positive context. "Not because you are more numerous than all the peoples did G-d desire you and choose you...Rather...because He observes the oath that He swore to your forefathers" (*Deuteronomy* 7:7-8). Or, "Do not say 'Because of my righteousness did G-d bring me to possess this Land...(It is) in order to establish the word that G-d swore to your forefathers, to Abraham, Isaac and Jacob'" (ibid. 9:4-5).

The concept of *zechus avos* (in the merit of one's ancestors) is repeatedly mentioned in Torah. Just as a wealthy person may bequeath his riches to his children, so have the Patriarchs bequeathed their spiritual treasures and merits to us. What is so unique about the verse in

Leviticus is that it occurs in the context of the *Tochachah* (Admonition), in which Moses tells the Israelites the horrendous punishments that will befall them if they deviate from faith in G-d and the observance of Torah. The comforting heritage of the Patriarchs appears to be out of place amidst the narration of the severe chastisement of the *Tochachah*.

The *Shelah* offers this example in explanation. Two people appeared before a judge, accused of stealing. The first man had been raised in an abusive home. His parents were dissolute people who neglected and abused him. He was not given a proper education. The people in his environment were corrupt and immoral. The second man grew up in a well-to-do family. His parents were honorable people who showered him with much love and the finest education.

The judge ordered the first man to be sent to a rehabilitation center, but gave the second man a harsh prison sentence. The latter protested his sentence as being unfair. "Why am I being punished so much more severely than this other man?" he complained.

The judge responded, "This other man never knew any better. All he saw during his growing years was criminal behavior. To him, stealing was normal. He never understood that it is wrong to steal. If he is taught right from wrong, he may correct his behavior. That is why I am sending him to a rehabilitation program. But you *were* taught right from wrong. Your parents were models of correct behavior. Your criminal behavior is inexcusable, and that is why you deserve to be punished."

This, the *Shelah* says, is why the Patriarchs are mentioned in the *Tochachah*. If we deviate from Torah, our punishment will be most severe because G-d will say, "Look who your ancestors were: Abraham, Isaac and Jacob were your models of absolute devotion to G-d. They withstood the severest of trials and remained faithful to G-d. With ancestors such as these, your deviance from Torah is inexcusable, and you will be dealt with more harshly."

Yes, *yichus* can be a liability.

But *yichus* can be a great asset if we incorporate the teachings and lifestyles of our forebears in our lives. In order to do so, we must know how they lived and their devotion to G-d and His Torah.

At first, my thought was to jot down stories about my great-grandfather, R' Mordechai Dov of Hornosetipol, affectionately known in the family as "the Zeide R' Motele" for my grandchildren and great-grandchildren. Then it occurred to me that I have profited greatly from stories about the great *tzaddikim* to whom I am not related. Why not share the stories about this remarkable *tzaddik* with others who may profit from them?

And so I present to you whatever I know about the Zeide R' Motele.

Yaakov Yisroel Kanievsky, the Steipler Gaon, derives his appelation from his origin in Hornosteipol. It may have been a bit difficult to pronounce "Hornosteipler," so it was abbreviated to "Steipler."

Whenever I visited the Steipler, I was warmly received. I had a correspondence with him for over twenty years. I published his Torah commentaries in *Yeamer LeYaakov UleYisroel*. Both he and my father were named Yaakov Yisroel after Zeide R' Motele's grandfather, the Cherkassy Zeide. They spent their boyhood years together and were on first name terms.

The Steipler's father, R' Chaim Peretz, served as a *shochet* in a village near Hornosteipel, and would visit Zeide R' Motele to learn Torah. When he was sixty, his wife died. Inasmuch as he had no male descendants (he had three daughters), he asked Zeide R' Motele whether he should remarry. Upon Zeide R' Motele's advice, he married a woman from Hornosteipel, who bore him three sons. Zeide R' Motele served as the *sandek* at the *bris* of the oldest son, and named him Yaakov Yisroel after the Zeide of Cherkassy. He blessed the infant that he would become a *gadol b'Yisrael*.

In one of his letters, the Steipler asked if I could send him the *sefer Emek Tefillah*, containing the teachings of the Cherkassy Zeide: "This *sefer* was my first source of *yiras shamayim* (fear of Heaven)." In one of his letters he writes, "I have received the holy *sefer Shosanas Haamakim* (comprised of the Cherkassy Zeide's *Emek Tefillah* and Zeide R' Motele's *Emek Chochmah*) for which I longed for many years. My first knowledge of fear of G-d was rooted in me by my father from this *sefer*, which he learned with me every Shabbos." After Zeide R' Motele died, R' Chaim Peretz became a *chassid* of his son, Zeide R' Leibele.

The Steipler discouraged having his picture taken, but granted me a special favor, which came about this way.

The Steipler Gaon with the author

When I visited the Steipler in 1965, I asked permission to have his picture taken, but he was reluctant to do so. I then asked permission to relate something my father had told me.

At one of the gatherings of the *gedolei Torah*, a photographer tried to get pictures of them. This was many years before the candid camera, and taking a picture required setting up an apparatus. It was simple to avoid having one's picture taken. The Gaon of Rogachow, R' Yoseph Rosen, resisted being photographed.

R' Meir Shapiro of Lublin approached the Gaon. "Apparently you have overlooked a Midrash," he said.

"What Midrash?" the Gaon asked, who knew the entire Midrash by heart.

"The Midrash says that G-d etched the image of the Patriarch Jacob on His throne," R' Meir said. "What was the purpose of that? G-d knew that there would be a time when the image of a true Jew would be a rarity. Because He desired to see what a true Jew should look like, He perpetuated the Patriarch's image.

"And I tell you," R' Meir continued, "that there will be days when people will not know what a true Jew should look like. This is why you should allow your picture to be taken." The Gaon consented, and we have a picture of him.

When I related this story to the Steipler, he smiled and said, "*Nu*, for you." My son then took this picture.

Like many of the *tzaddikim* of his time, Zeide R' Motele did not allow himself to be photographed. He told his *chassidim* not to try to photograph him, because they would not succeed.

One Purim, as Zeide R' Motele was sitting at his table, a *chassid* came in and said, "Rebbe, because of you I am unable to marry off my children."

Zeide R' Motele responded with wonderment, "Because of me?"

"I am a photographer," the *chassid* said. "If you would allow me to take your picture, I could sell it and earn enough to marry off my children."

Zeide R' Motele's compassion overcame his resistance. "Who is stopping you?" he said.

The photographer then took the only pictures we have of Zeide R' Motele.

Chapter 1
The Closer to Us,
the More Impressive

On my trips to Eretz Yisrael, I visited the burial sites of our great *tzaddikim*. I prayed at the tombs of the Patriarchs, Abraham, Isaac and Jacob in Chebron, at the tombs of the authors of the Mishnah in Tzefas and of R' Meir Baal Haness and of the Rambam in Teveryah. I noticed something rather odd. I thought I would be moved the most in Chebron at the tombs of the Patriarchs, but that did not happen. I was more emotionally moved at the site of the Ari z"l and even more at the graves of the disciples of the Baal Shem Tov.

I reflected upon this and concluded that the vast gap in time between myself and the Patriarchs resulted in an emotional distancing. The closer the *tzaddik* was to my own time, the stronger was the relationship. Among the disciples of the Baal Shem Tov there were some very familiar names of *tzaddikim* who were just several generations away. I knew people who knew people who had seen them and lived with them, and this made them more real to me.

The one exception was at the tomb of the Matriarch Rachel. Although she was as remote as the Patriarchs, the emotion was most intense. But that, of course, is because she was our mother. When one approaches her tombstone and hears the supplicants cry, "Mama!" the gap in time fades into nothingness.

I feel a similar phenomenon in relationship to our great *tzaddikim*. The greatest of all is, of course, Moshe *Rabbeinu*, our eternal teacher. Even in his own time, Moses was so far above everyone else that the Israelites' great reverence for him did not translate into the kinship and affection that they felt for the High Priest, Aaron (*Rashi, Deuteronomy* 34:8). The prophets and the authors of the Talmud are so far above us that it is difficult to feel a closeness to them. "If the earlier *tzaddikim* were angels, then by comparison we are mortals" (*Shabbos* 112b). It is difficult for a mortal to identify with angels. This holds true for the *tzaddikim* of subsequent generations as well. They were so great that they are almost unreal.

As we approach our own times, the emotional closeness increases. My first Talmud teacher studied under the Chafetz Chaim. He was able to tell me about this exceptional human being, and I could think of him as a flesh-and-blood angel. I knew people who knew the *tzaddik* of Sanz, the Sfas Emes and the Imrei Emes of Gur, R' Chaim Ozer Grodzinski of Vilna and many other Torah giants. They are more real to me. Their extraordinary greatness notwithstanding, I can feel closer to them than to their forebears.

Because of the myriad stories told about the *chassid*ic masters, Chassidus has sometimes been referred to as "legendary reality." There is no denying that Chassidus brought about a cataclysmic change in Jewish life, and the extraordinary powers of the *tzaddikim* brought about this change. *Chassidim* revel in relating miracles wrought by the Rebbes. The Rebbe of Rhizin is alleged to have said, "Anyone who believes that all the miraculous stories told about the Baal Shem Tov are factual is credulous. Anyone who thinks they could not have occurred is guilty of apostasy."

That statement may hold true for the *tzaddikim* of past generations with whom we had no direct contact. They may be thought of as "legendary reality." The closer we get to our own times, the less "legendary" they are and the more real they are.

One of the Rebbes of whom I will be relating stories is R' Mordechai, the Maggid of Czernoble, who died in 5597 (1835).

In 1927, my father was in Montreal. When the word got around that the Hornosteipol Rebbe was in town, people who came from around the Kiev area gathered to meet him. One man, who was eighty-six years old, was from this area of the Ukraine. After talking to my father a bit, he asked, "Rabbi, would you mind going to visit my father?"

My father was surprised that an octogenarian's father was living. "How old is your father?" he asked.

"He claims he is one hundred twelve," the man said, "but he is denying his age. We know for a fact that he is one hundred fourteen."

Of course, my father seized the opportunity. The centenarian was in a home for the aged, physically frail but mentally alert. The man who accompanied my father said, "R' Shlomo, I'd like to have your longevity."

The old man replied, "Never mind. You can have your own longevity. I will keep mine." He then told my father that he had visited the Maggid of Czernoble, my father's ancestor of five generations earlier. This man was twenty-two when the Maggid died.

My father used to frequently relate his encounter with a person who had been in the presence of the Maggid. He also loved to tell that before he left, the centenarian asked him, "Did my boychickl come to see you?" My father pointed out that to a parent, a child is always a child, a "boychickl" even at eighty-six. Incidentally, the man died a year later, and the Prime Minister attended the funeral of Canada's oldest citizen.

The proximity to Zeide R' Motele is why he occupies so significant a position in my life. Although my father knew him only in his childhood, my older aunts and uncles knew him well. I was close with my Zeide R' Leibele, his son and successor. I knew many people who were his *chassidim*. Zeide R' Motele is very, very real to me, and his impact upon me has been most profound.

I know that when I pray the *Amidah* (*Shemoneh Esrei*) and say *zocher chasdei avos*, that G-d recalls the kindnesses of our ancestors, I should be thinking of the Patriarchs, Abraham, Isaac and Jacob. But try as I might, I cannot help but think of my ancestor, the Zeide R' Motele.

History has had people who did not belong in their generation. In the secular world, Leonardo da Vinci was centuries ahead of his time. A similar phenomenon occurs in the Torah world, but in reverse chronology. There were Torah personalities who did not belong in their generation because they were of the caliber of the *tzaddikim* of earlier centuries. The Gaon of Vilna and the Gaon of Rogachow could have been peers of Torah scholars several centuries before them.

Zeide R' Motele was such a phenomenon. When he visited his great uncle, the Rebbe of Talna, the latter escorted him saying, "Young and old. Old and young." *Chassidim* asked the Rebbe what he meant by this. He replied, "Young Rebbes should sit at his feet and learn from him. Old Rebbes should visit him and hang their heads in shame that a young man has so surpassed them and has reached such amazing spiritual heights."

Zeide R' Motele's astounding Torah scholarship can be seen from his halachic works, especially *Chibur LeTaharah* on the laws of mikvah and *netilas yadayim* (hand-washing before eating) which he wrote at age eighteen. It is related that when the great Talmudist, R' Chaim of Brisk, read this work he remarked that he did not think that there was anyone in this generation who was capable of composing it. His other important halachic works are responsa, *Emek Shailah*, and *Turei Zahav* on the laws of *ribbis* (usury).

Zeide R' Motele maintained a halachic correspondence with his father-in-law, the great gaon, R' Chaim Halberstam of Sanz. In one letter Zeide R' Motele wrote to his father-in-law, "Undoubtedly, because throngs of people constantly besiege you with their requests for your help, you did not have the time to look closely at my writings." Upon receipt of this letter, the Sanzer *tzaddik* said, "Our R' Motele is accusing us that we do not learn properly. True, to learn Torah *lishmah* (solely as a mitzvah) the way he does is beyond us. His Torah illuminates the heavens. Nevertheless, we do learn something."

For me, this outstanding *tzaddik* has been an important if not the primary source for reinforcing my *emunah* (faith). The human mind cannot escape questioning, and the *yetzer hara* is adept at introducing doubts in everyone's mind. There are many questions that go unanswered, and these can challenge one's *emunah* and *bitachon* (trust in G-d). For example, the mystery of why righteous people

Chibur LeTaharah, sefer by Zeide Reb Motele

suffer can eat away at a person, and even Moses was not granted insight into this mystery. Our convictions of *emunah* may be threatened by the repeated sufferings that Jews have experienced throughout history. Why does G-d, Whose benevolence is infinite, allow these to happen?

Whenever I am bothered by such questions and doubts, I think, "These are hardly new questions. Zeide R' Motele was as familiar with them as I am, and his wisdom was so much greater than mine. If he remained steadfast in his *emunah*, who am I to allow these questions to undermine my *emunah*?"

The *midrashim* regarding Moses indeed point out that he acknowledged the justice of G-d even though he did not understand it. This is equally true of the authors of the Talmud. Their unshakeable *emunah* should quash all skepticism. But they were so distant, so long ago, that I cannot reach out to them for all the strength I need. But Zeide R' Motele? He is so close to me through all who knew him personally. I can reach out to him, and he provides the reassurance I need.

I hope he can do the same for you.

Chapter 2
The Origins of a *Tzaddik*:
R' Zusia of Anipoli

Whatever one may think of *yichus*, we should understand that not only does a person's immediate family impact upon his character, but so does one's remote family. We absorb values and philosophies of life from our ancestors. A comprehensive portrait of Zeide R' Motele, therefore, requires knowing something about his *yichus*. I will narrate some stories about his forebears. Several of these may have appeared elsewhere in my writings, but I must include them for the sake of completion.

I am going to go beyond an accounting of *yichus* that was interrupted by the *tzaddik* of Sanz. That happened in this way.

> Before Zeide R' Motele's marriage to the Sanzer *tzaddik's* daughter, Raitza, the *tzaddik* said to Zeide R' Motele's grandfather, the Rebbe of Cherkassy, "It is customary to relate the *yichus* before the wedding. The *kallah* is a descendant of R' Boruch Frankel (author of Boruch Taam), the *Chacham Tzvi*, the *Maginei Shlomo*, the *Megalle Amukos*, the *Maharshal*," and continued to name many more Torah luminaries.

When his turn came, the Rebbe of Cherkassy said, "The *choson* is a descendant of R' Zusia of Anipoli …"

The *tzaddik* of Sanz interrupted him. "Enough!" he said. "There is no need to continue further."

The *tzaddik* of Sanz explained, "There is nothing to add to the Rebbe R' Zusia," and related the following story.

> *The great Maggid, R' Dov Ber of Mezeritch, would fast most of the week. In his old age, the disciples were concerned that his health was being affected by his fasting, and they appointed R' Zusia to plead with the Maggid to discontinue his fasting.*
>
> *When R' Zusia carried the message to the Maggid, the latter responded, "You are telling me not to fast? Why, you fast from Shabbos to Shabbos! If you will agree to eat on any yoma depagra (special festive days), I will stop fasting." R' Zusia readily agreed.*
>
> *On one of the special days, R' Zusia went into the kitchen and asked for some food. The cook said that she had nothing to give him and would have to go buy some food to prepare. However, she could not leave her infant unattended. R' Zusia offered to watch the baby while she left.*
>
> *R' Zusia sat by the baby's crib, studying the sefer of the Shelah (R' Yeshaya Halevi). When the baby began crying, R' Zusia put the book aside and began rocking the cradle. The holy Shelah came down from Gan Eden (Paradise) and said to him, "I will rock the cradle. You go back to learning my sefer."*

The *tzaddik* of Sanz said, "With an ancestor whose learning was so holy as to bring down the *Shelah* from *Gan Eden,* there is no need to go any further."

I know that there are skeptics who will raise their eyebrows at this story. I can only react with the story of the Chafetz Chaim, who had to appear as a character witness in a trial.

When he declined to be sworn in because he never took an oath, the attorney told the judge that he may waive the oath, because the Chafetz Chaim is incapable of deviating from the truth.

The attorney told the judge that the Chafetz Chaim once noticed a thief walking off with his candlesticks. He promptly called out in a loud voice that he abandoned his ownership of the candlesticks so that the thief would not be committing theft. "A man like that does not lie," the attorney said.

The judge responded, "Do you expect me to believe that story?"

The attorney answered, "Your Honor, they do not tell stories like that about you or me."

The stories told about a person are a testimony to his character, whether or not they are factual.

I heard many stories from my father about R' Zusia. This is one of his favorites.

During the self-imposed exile that he undertook along with his brother, the *tzaddik* R' Elimelech of Lizhenzsk, they once lodged at an inn where the only available sleeping places were on two shelves. At night the villagers came in and indulged in drink. When they became tipsy, they danced around in a circle, and each time they danced past the two sleeping men, one of the revelers landed a heavy blow on R' Zusia.

R' Elimelech said, "My brother, why should you absorb all the beatings? Let us change places."

After they changed places and the tipsy batterer was about to land another blow, a comrade said to him, "Why are you always hitting the one on the bottom shelf? Why don't you hit the one on the top shelf, too?" which he promptly did.

R' Zusia said to his brother, "You see, Melech, if it is *bashert* (destined) for Zusia to be beaten, there is no way of escaping it."

I think this was my father's way of telling me, "You can't outsmart what is *bashert* for you."

Among the disciples of the Maggid of Mezeritch there were several whose enormous Talmudic erudition is evident from their halachic writings, such as R' Pinchos Horowitz, author of *Haflaah* and R' Shneur Zalman, whose "Shulchan Aruch" is a classic text frequently referred to in the *Mishnah Berurah*. R' Zusia, however, was rarely seen to be studying Talmud. Usually he was sweeping the floor of the Beis Midrash or stoking the fire in the furnace. Yet, R' Shneur Zalman referred to R' Zusia as the "true gaon." The reason for that can be seen from the following story.

A man approached R' Zusia with this problem. His late father, who had been a pious Jew, regularly appeared to him in a dream, urging him to convert to Christianity. R' Zusia told the man to return in a few days for an answer. During the next few days, R' Zusia fasted and prayed intensely. When the man returned, R' Zusia told him that one of the caretakers at the cemetery had been wearing a cross which had fallen into his father's grave. The grave was opened and indeed, a cross was found and removed, after which there was no recurrence of the dream.

The report of this incident came to the ears of the Gaon of Vilna, who was not surprised. "An incident like that is recorded in the Jerusalem Talmud." When the comment of the Gaon was reported to R' Zusia, he said, "I am not a scholar, and I was not aware of the passage in the Jerusalem Talmud, but I knew this from the same source that the authors of the Jerusalem Talmud did."

R' Shneur Zalman said, "When R' Zusia finds that he cannot understand a commentary of the Talmud, he prays and cries so intensely that the author of that commentary reveals himself to him and explains it himself." He said that R' Zusia is, therefore, a "true gaon," because he gets his information from the source.

The Maggid of Mezeritch once told the Alter Rebbe (R' Shneur Zalman, author of *Tanya*) to see if it would be possible to devise a form of the script for the parchments of the *tefillin* that would reconcile and satisfy the specifications of both R'

Yoseph Karo and the Ari z"l. The Alter Rebbe spent countless hours on this task, and finally brought a script to the Maggid which satisfied the divergent opinions. The Maggid was elated. "Take this script to R' Moshe (the *sofer* [scribe]) of Pschevorsk and ask him to write parchments of *tefillin* for me with this script." Upon reaching R' Moshe, the Alter Rebbe was astonished to find him writing parchments with the new script he had devised. "Where did you get that script?" the Alter Rebbe asked. R' Moshe answered, "Zusia brought me this script yesterday." How did R' Zusia get this script? Hardly a challenge for someone who can get the authors of *tosafos* (Talmud commentaries) to explain their words.

This is reminiscent of the story in the Talmud, that when the son of R' Yochanan ben Zakkai fell ill, he asked R' Chanina ben Dosa to pray for him. After a brief prayer the child recovered, leading R' Yochanan to say, "If I prayed intensely all day, I would not have achieved what R' Chanina did in his brief prayer." R' Yochanan's wife said, "Does that mean that Chanina is a greater Torah scholar than you?" R' Yochanan replied, "No, but whereas I have the status of a minister in a royal court who has access to the king only by appointment, Chanina is like a servant in the palace, who can enter the king's chambers at any time" (*Berachos* 34b).

The Talmud relates a similar comment about Choni Hamaagel (Choni of the circle), whose appellation resulted from an incident when he was asked to pray for rain. Choni drew a circle on the ground and stood within it, saying, "Master of the Universe! Your children asked me to intercede for them. I swear by Your holy Name that I will not step out of this circle until You have mercy on them." Immediately it began to rain. R' Shimon ben Shotach said, "If you were not Choni, I would have excommunicated you for the audacity of confronting G-d. But what can I do? You are like a child who can get anything from his father when he cries for it" (*Taanis* 19a).

R' Zusia always reminded me of these great *tzaddikim*, whose prayers were so effective.

There was a further similarity to R' Chanina ben Dosa, of whom the Talmud says, "The entire world is sustained by the merits of R' Chanina ben Dosa, but for himself, a small measure of carob is enough to satisfy him for an entire week" (*Taanis* 24b). R' Zusia prayed for others, but his own needs were sparse. He lived in abject poverty.

> Despite his poverty, R' Zusia was always in high spirit. Someone asked him, "How can you be happy when your wife and children are so miserable with their poverty?" R' Zusia answered, "How can they not be miserable, when they depend on a ne'r-do-well like Zusia for their sustenance? But I depend for my sustenance on G-d, Who can give me everything I need."

The key to R' Zusia is his understanding of his needs. Someone asked him, "How can you, in good faith, recite the *berachah* (blessing) thanking G-d 'Who is providing me my every need' when you are lacking in everything?" R' Zusia shrugged. "G-d knows what my needs are better than I do. He knows that one of my needs is poverty, so he provides me with that."

> A *chassid* asked the Maggid to explain the Talmudic ruling that a person should thank G-d for the bad things that happen to him just as he would for the good things (*Berachos* 54a). How can that be expected of a person? The Maggid said, "Go over to the man who is sweeping the floor and ask him."
>
> When the man told R' Zusia that he could not understand the passage in the Talmud, R' Zusia said, "I cannot help you. I am not a Talmudic scholar." The man insisted that the Maggid had directed him to him for an answer and posed his question. R' Zusia answered, "How could I possibly answer your question? I have never had anything bad happen to me." The man looked at R' Zusia, whose tattered clothes testified to his abject poverty, and he had the answer to his question.

> R' Yisroel of Rhizin said that R' Zusia did not transmit many of the teachings of the Maggid of Mezeritch. When the Maggid

began his discourse, "And G-d said," R' Zusia was overcome by an ecstatic fervor and started shouting, "G-d said, G-d said!" and caused such commotion that he had to be escorted from the room. He would stand in the hall, beating his hands against the wall and shouting, "G-d said!" He never heard a complete discourse. "However," R' Yisroel said, "If a person listens in the spirit of truth and speaks in the spirit of truth, he can uplift and redeem the entire world with a single word. That was R' Zusia's greatness."

R' Zusia received occasional support from a wealthy follower. One time this man came to Anipoli and was told that R' Zusia was in Mezeritch at his Rebbe. The man reasoned, "If R' Zusia has a Rebbe, he must be an even greater *tzaddik* than he is, then I should give my support to him." When he found that his fortunes began to dwindle, he returned to R' Zusia who explained, "G-d relates to us as we do to others. When you saw fit to give to someone as devoid of merits as Zusia, G-d gave you wealth without examining whether you deserved it or not. But when you chose to give only to a *tzaddik* of great merit, then G-d examined whether you merit His bounty."

One of R' Zusia's well known statements is, "When I will be asked on Judgment Day why I was not as great as the Baal Shem Tov, I will say 'How could you expect that of me?' If they will ask me why I was not as great as the Maggid, I will say, 'How could you expect that of me?' But when they will say, 'But Zusia, why were you not as great as Zusia could have been?' woe is to me! For that I will have no answer."

There are many stories about the two brothers, the *tzaddikim* R' Elimelech of Lizhenzsk and R' Zusia of Anipoli. R' Zusia was actually the one who brought R' Elimelech to the Maggid of Mezeritch. R' Elimelech was a great Talmudic scholar, and asked his brother, "Zusia, why do you spend so much time praying? Why don't you spend more time studying Torah?" R' Zusia answered with a parable.

A simple person, a woodcutter, developed a strong desire to see the king. He wandered from village to village, finally arriving at the capital city. He found his way to the palace, and stood outside the palace gate, hoping to get a glimpse of the king when he left the palace.

After several days, the guard at the palace gate asked him why he was standing there. The woodcutter told him that this was his only hope of getting a glimpse of the king. Seeing the man's sincerity, he allowed him to enter the palace courtyard, where he again took up a vigil.

Before long, one of the officers in the courtyard asked him what he was doing there, and being impressed with the man's sincerity, took him into the palace. He eventually arranged to be allowed to heat the palace by making the fires. The word got around to the king that he had a subject who was totally devoted, and the king summoned him to the throne room.

"I see that you are sincerely devoted to me," the king said. "Do you have any wish that I can grant you?"

The man answered, "I know that I am a simple person and do not deserve to be in Your Majesty's presence. But perhaps I could have a room with a window overlooking the entrance to the throne room, so that I could see Your Majesty come and go." The king granted his request.

One time, the king's son committed an offense, for which he was banished from the palace for a year. He longed to be back in the palace, and upon meeting the woodcutter, asked him to give him his woodsman's clothes. "That way I will be able to get into your room and see my father."

The woodsman said, "No, that is not fitting for you. You are the prince, and you deserve to be in the king's presence constantly. All you must do is ask your father's forgiveness and pledge not to repeat your errant behavior, and you will be warmly received. But I have no claim to be in the king's presence. All I can do is watch him from my little room."

"You see, Elimelech, you are a great Torah scholar. Your vast knowledge of the Torah endears you to G-d, and you are like a prince in the royal court. But me? I am unlearned and I have no claim to be permitted in the King's presence. If I do not pray fervently and stoke the fires of heaven with prayer, how shall I ever get close to the King?"

By looking at a person, R' Zusia was able to detect the wrongdoings he had committed. Speaking to himself, he would then say, "Zusia, Zusia! What is it with you that you have been so sinful? Just look at what you have done!" Then he would go on to castigate himself for all the wrongdoings the other person had done. Invariably, this would penetrate to the person's heart and result in his doing *teshuvah*.

One time, however, R' Zusia saw a sinful person approach the Maggid, and he was infuriated. How dare a person approach the holy Maggid without first doing *teshuvah*! He could not contain himself and sharply chastised the man. A bit later he regretted this, and asked the Maggid to divest him of the ability to see the wrongs a person had done. After this, R' Zusia saw only the good in people.

One time, a follower of R' Zusia gave him ten rubles, for safekeeping. R' Zusia put the money into a volume of the Bible, on the page that said, "You shall not steal." Later he found that someone had taken five rubles and had put the remaining five rubles on the page that read, "You shall love your neighbor as yourself." Upon discovering the theft, R' Zusia said, "Master of the universe! See how wonderful Your children are. Zusia was so selfish, keeping the whole ten rubles for himself. The needy person who took the money was much more considerate. He fulfilled the mitzvah of 'Love your neighbor' and shared the money with Zusia."

Some of R' Zusia's comments on Torah have been preserved. R' Zusia cited the verse: "G-d said, take for Me an offering (*Exodus* 25:2)." It would have been more appropriate to say, "*Give* me an offering." R' Zusia explained that it is not too difficult to be a donor or benefactor. A person feels elevated when one does something for others. It is much more difficult to be a recipient of someone's beneficence. One may feel humiliated by being the recipient of help, and one may not be grateful or may even develop a resentment towards one's benefactor. The Torah teaches us that we must learn how to accept as well as how to give, hence "Take for Me" rather than "Give to Me."

The Talmud says that one who answers "Amen" should not raise his voice above the one who recites the blessing (*Berachos* 45a). R' Zusia commented, "It is the *neshamah* that recites the blessing. The body responds to the *neshamah's* words. We must be cautious that the body's response should not overwhelm and drown out the *neshamah*."

> R' Zusia once said to his brother, R' Elimelech, "Melech, I am tormented by a problem. The Talmud says that the souls of all humans until the end of time were contained in the soul of Adam. Then you and I were there, too. How did we allow Adam to transgress the Divine command and eat of the forbidden fruit?"
>
> R' Elimelech responded, "I did want to resist, but I realized that the serpent had told Adam and Eve that G-d forbade the fruit of the Tree of Knowledge because, if they ate from its fruit, they would be as wise as G-d (*Genesis* 3:5). If Adam had not eaten of it, he might have thought for the rest of his life, 'If only I had eaten the fruit, I would have been as wise as G-d.' I, therefore, decided that it would be far better to let him transgress than to live his entire life with the heretical thought that a human being can be as wise as G-d."
>
> R' Zusia responded, "You have given me peace of mind. A person must realize that even with the maximum wisdom attainable, one is nothing before the Infinite."

It was to R' Zusia that the Maggid taught that he should learn three things from observing an infant: (1) An infant is always happy, (2) an infant is never idle, and (3) when an infant wants something, it cries until the parents fulfill its needs. Little wonder that R' Zusia was able to achieve the true meaning of the *tosafos*. The Maggid had told him to cry until he gets what he wants. Could R' Zusia not have used the same technique to improve his wretched lot? Of course, but it had never occurred to him that he needed anything more than he had.

Yes, R' Zusia cried for whatever he really wanted. At the end of the day, he would write down whatever improper things he had done or whatever improper thoughts he had, then he would cry over them until his tears erased the writing. Yet, when he finished crying, R' Zusia was as happy as an infant.

On his deathbed, the first of the disciples that the Maggid asked for was R' Zusia. He held R' Zusia's hand and said, "Zusia, you were mine in this world, and in the next world you will be together with me."

Even if the *Shelah* had not come down from Gan Eden so that R' Zusia could study his work, what we know about R' Zusia would have sufficed to explain why the *tzaddik* of Sanz felt that no further elaboration of *yichus* was needed.

R' Zusia of Anipoli was the grandfather of R' Michel of Karima, whose wife, Bela, was a descendant of R' Zvi Ashkenzi (Chacham Zvi). Both via Bela and via R' Shneur Zalman, Zeide R' Motele was a descendant of the MaHaral of Prague. R' Michel was the father of R' Zusia of Tolumutsch, who was Zeide R' Motele's father.

Chapter 3
The Origin of Chassidus and the Baal Shem Tov Legacy

I do not intend this to be a treatise on Chassidus, but a few words about Chassidus are essential in order to have an understanding of Zeide R' Motele.

Although Zeide R' Motele was a descendant of the Baal Shem Tov, it is difficult to lay any special claim to this lineage. All Rebbes and all *chassidim* can trace themselves to the Baal Shem Tov. As R' Shneur Zalman once said to the Baal Shem Tov's grandson, R' Baruch of Medzhibozh, "Just as he is your physical zeide, he is my spiritual zeide."

A few words about the development of Chassidus are in order.

The Baal Shem Tov was born in 5458 (1698). The plight of the Jews in Russia-Poland at that time was lamentable. Both the Russian and Polish governments were fiercely anti-Semitic and their hatred for and persecution of Jews was consistently fomented and fueled by the Church, which wielded enormous power. Jews were generally deprived of civil-liberties. They were not permitted to live in major cities without special permission. This resulted in the development of the *shtetl* (village) culture. They were not permitted access to the professions or educational institutions. They were at the mercy of the local *poritz* (feudal lord), who was not answerable to any authority, and who had life-and-death powers over his vassals. Blood libel plots were frequent, and pogroms occurred at the whim of anyone who wished to discharge his rage or to enrich himself at the expense of helpless Jews.

No sooner had the massacres of the Crusades subsided, than a vicious and widespread pogrom broke out in 5408 (1648) under the leadership of Chmielniecki, decimating entire villages. These pitiful conditions fired the hope for a miraculous redemption, and in 1665, Shabbetai Zevi declared himself as Mashiach, who would liberate the Jews and return them to their homeland.

Shabbetai Zevi was apparently a Talmudic scholar, in Smyrna, Turkey, who had become immersed in Kabbalah. He was very charismatic, and had the delusion that he was Mashiach. He abrogated the fast days of mourning for the destruction of the Temple. His conviction of his Messianic mission and his charisma, coupled with the intense hope of people desperate for salvation from their misery, resulted in his attracting a large following, which included some of the noted Torah authorities of the time. Alarmed by Shabbetai Zevi's activities, the Turkish authorities threatened to kill him unless he converted to Islam, and he chose the latter option. His defection to Islam punctured the balloon of imminent salvation, and sent Eastern European Jewry into a tailspin of utter despair.

Community institutions were decimated by the repeated pogroms, and the social and economic decline resulted in severe deterioration of education. Not too many people could afford to receive a proper Torah education. Children in *cheder* (Hebrew school) learned how to read and studied the Bible. Some people had a smattering of Talmud, but true scholarship was rather uncommon. The learned elite tended to look down upon the unlearned masses. Indeed, the Talmud says, "Why is it unusual for the sons of Torah scholars to become scholars? Because they (the parents) refer to the common folk as donkeys" (*Nedarim* 81a).

This was the scene that the Baal Shem Tov came upon: oppression, discrimination, depression and despair. There are countless stories about the Baal Shem Tov as a miracle worker, but they are not germane here. What is important is that he undertook to inject life, hope and *simchah* (joy) into Jewish life. Given the deplorable conditions under which Eastern European Jews lived, bringing them out of despair and injecting *simchah* into their lives was probably the greatest miracle the Baal Shem Tov performed. It may be said that the Baal Shem Tov rejuvenated Judaism.

The term "rejuvenated" is important. The Baal Shem Tov did not see himself as an innovator. On a number of occasions the Talmud refers to a particular practice as, "It had been forgotten, and the sages reinstated it" (*Succah* 44a).

The Baal Shem Tov taught that the service of G-d is not to be compartmentalized. In contrast to those who saw withdrawal from the world and total immersion into spirituality as desirable, the Baal Shem Tov emphasized the Talmudic principle (*Berachos* 63a) that one must cleave unto G-d in everything one does (*Proverbs* 3:6). Worldly activities need not detract one from the Divine service. "If one studies the Torah laws regarding commercial transactions, one is doing a mitzvah. It is no less of a mitzvah if one engages in commerce and *applies* the laws of Torah to his activities."

The Talmud states that if a person was born with a tendency to shed blood, he should have an occupation where this trait can be constructive, such as a *shochet* (ritual slaughterer) or *mohel* (one who performs circumcisions) (*Shabbos* 156a). In other words, provide a constructive outlet for a character trait that could be destructive. This is similar to the psychological defense mechanism of *sublimation*, with one important difference. Psychologically, sublimation occurs at a subconscious level. If a person has an urge which the super-ego or conscience condemns as unacceptable, the subconscious mind channels it into an acceptable behavior. However, this takes place *without the person being aware of the unacceptable drive and its transformation.* The astronomer who examines the skies by peering through a telescope is unaware that the origin of his behavior is voyeurism, and that his subconscious mind has made the transformation from destructive curiosity to constructive curiosity.

The Talmudic statement is different. It states that a person *who is aware of a destructive drive should make a conscious decision to direct it into constructive behavior.* This may seem to be a subtle difference, but it is an extremely important one and serves as the basis for one of the Baal Shem Tov's major teachings.

Without the Divine spirit which G-d instituted into humans, man would be just another animal. The human body has all the physical urges and drives of an animal. Many of these are morally and socially so reprehensible that the subconscious mind takes them out of awareness. This is the psychological mechanism of *repression*. It is important to note that repression occurs subconsciously, without a person being aware that it is happening. Repression can be thought of as the lid of a jack-in-the-box. The figurine inside the box sits on a coiled spring which tries to push it up, and if the lid is lifted, the figurine pops up. Similarly, a repressed drive tries to push itself into one's awareness and to become active. *Keeping an idea repressed requires psychic energy.* It can be thought of as if the catch on the lid of the jack-in-the-box were broken, and one must exert energy to depress the coiled spring in order to keep the figurine contained within the box. This exertion of energy must be constant, because any let up would permit its coming into awareness. Furthermore, a repressed idea can find ways of circumventing the conscience and emerging into pathological behavior.

Emotions are energy. Subduing an emotion requires exertion of energy. The Baal Shem Tov taught that repression is a wasteful expenditure of energy. There is no need to banish an unacceptable idea from one's awareness. It is a natural component of man's physical nature. Rather, a person should be aware of it and do as the Talmud says; i.e., *consciously and volitionally sublimate it.* A reprehensible idea which is relegated to the subconscious remains an unknown enemy, and one cannot do battle to subdue an unknown enemy. Recognizing that a human being may have many animalistic drives and *consciously* channeling and transforming these drives can conserve an enormous amount of psychic energy. In this way, all of a person's drives can be channeled into constructive outlets. The Baal Shem Tov interpreted the verse, "Turn from evil and do good" (*Psalms* 34:15) as meaning "turn away from evil by transforming it into good." Chassidus thus integrated all of a person's life into the Divine service. As we shall later see, differences of opinion arose among chassidic teachers on how this should be accomplished.

One of the changes the Baal Shem Tov suggested was to do away with self-imposed fasting as a method of *teshuvah.* "It is much greater to make eating part of the Divine service than fasting. If a person eats not merely to please the palate but rather that the energy derived from the food should enable him to do the mitzvos properly, that transforms the mundane act of eating into a Divine service. All of life is to be hallowed, and all one's actions should be consecrated."

> Someone asked R' Elimelech of Lizhenzsk, "But did not the Baal Shem Tov himself fast prodigiously?" R' Elimelech replied, "After Shabbos, the Baal Shem Tov would go into the woods where he would meditate and pray in seclusion all week. He would take along six loaves of bread for the week. When he returned home on Friday, he found the sack to be heavy. On opening it, he was surprised to find the six loaves untouched. That kind of fasting is permissible."

The Baal Shem Tov's emphasis on "devotion of the heart" was hardly anything new. The Talmud states, "G-d desires the devotion of the heart" (*Sanhedrin* 106b). Performance of ritual mitzvos while neglecting *middos* (refined character traits) was denounced by the prophets. "Though you offer Me burnt-offerings and your meal-offerings, I will not accept them...Take away from Me the noise of your songs, and let Me not hear the melody of your prayers. But let justice well up as waters, and righteousness as a mighty stream" (*Amos* 5:22-24). These were traditional concepts which the Baal Shem Tov revitalized.

The psalmist says, "Serve G-d with joy" (*Psalms* 100:2). Chassidus sought to restore the joy whose role in Judaism is so important that Moses said that the worst travails that would befall Jews would be for not serving G-d with joy (*Deuteronomy* 28:47). The Baal Shem Tov taught that devotional joy is essential not only as an attitude for prayer, but in everything a person does. His passion in prayer and his own manifestation of joy served as a model for his disciples, whose personalities and teachings revived the aching hearts of Jews.

But how could one expect people who are so oppressed and persecuted to be joyous? The Baal Shem Tov had the answer.

The Midrash says that G-d created the world because, "He wished to have a presence in the lower world" (*Tanchuma, Bechukosai*). While we may not understand why G-d should wish that, the Talmud says that this is indeed so. We attract the imminent presence of G-d by performing His mitzvos. The Talmud also says that in *Gan Eden* the *neshamos* will have the incomparable bliss of basking in the radiance of the Divine glory.

The Baal Shem Tov pointed out that the Divine presence is as real in this world as it is in the celestial spheres, but that whereas it is manifest in *Gan Eden*, it is in a state of *hester* (concealment) in this earthly world. Although we are unable to perceive it, a firm belief in G-d's presence can undo the *hester*. We can then be, in this earthly world, in a state of bliss similar to that of *Gan Eden*. Awareness of this should give one a feeling of supreme exaltation. The elation of being in the immanent presence of G-d should be so great that it should obscure all earthly distresses and discomforts (*Tanya* 26).

In contrast to Shabbetai Zevi, who promised the joy of salvation only with the coming of Mashiach, the Baal Shem Tov taught that one can experience the joy of salvation even under the most trying circumstances. The attraction of the Divine presence into the earthly world by performance of the mitzvos is adequate reason for elation. "This," the Baal Shem Tov said, "is the meaning of the verse: 'Happy is the people who know the joyful shout, O G-d, they walk in the light of Your countenance' (*Psalms* 89:16). Knowing that one is always in the presence of the Divine light is cause for happiness."

Joy should pervade all the Divine service. Even solemnity can be joyous. The Baal Shem Tov said that he learned this from a cantor, who used to chant the *Al chet* (confession of one's sins) with a merry melody. When asked why he did so, the cantor said, "If I were assigned to sweep the dirt out of the palace to make it clean for the presence of the king, would I not be elated at the opportunity? When I confess my sins, I am cleansing myself for the G-dly soul to rest within me. That is an occasion for great joy."

One year at the end of Yom Kippur, when it is traditional to recite the Prayer for the New Moon, the sky was heavily overcast, and the Baal Shem Tov was despondent that he would not have the opportunity to perform this mitzvah. He prayed fervently for the skies to clear, but to no avail. The *chassidim*, unaware of the master's despondency, began singing and dancing, joyously celebrating the forgiveness G-d had granted them on Yom Kippur. They danced into the Baal Shem Tov's study and asked the Master to join them.

After a few minutes had passed, someone announced that there was a break in the clouds and the moon was visible. The Baal Shem Tov said that with their dancing, the *chassidim* had been able to achieve what his prayers had failed to accomplish.

Although the *tzaddik* was the inspiring leader, Chassidus taught that the *tzaddik* was as spiritually dependent on his followers as they were on him.

One time the Baal Shem Tov prayed the silent *Amidah* for an inordinately long time. Several of the disciples grew impatient and left, and the Baal Shem Tov abruptly concluded his prayer. He then gently reprimanded them, "If one wishes to reach a very high place, one may have to stand on the shoulders of someone who, in turn, is standing on another person's shoulders. If either of the bottom persons leave, the top person falls.

"As long as you were all with me, I could stand on your shoulders and reach the highest celestial spheres. When you left, I fell down."

The Baal Shem Tov pointed out that *deveikus* (cleaving to G-d) is the goal of Torah and mitzvos. The Baal Shem interpreted the verse, "And you who cleave unto your G-d" (*Deuteronomy* 4:4), as meaning "You cleave to G-d Who is within you." He cited the Talmud that "the Divine presence does not rest among sadness" (*Shabbos* 30b), hence joy is necessary to achieve *deveikus*.

The Baal Shem Tov was intolerant of *maggidim* (itinerant preachers) who admonished the congregates for their laxity in Torah study and proper performance of mitzvos. "Do you know," he said, "that when a Jew comes home after a hard day's work, exhausted and depressed because of his meager earnings and says, 'Oy! I have only a few minutes until sunset' and then rushes through *minchah* (afternoon prayer), do you know that the heavenly angels tremble before the holiness of his prayer?" In contrast to the teachings of the *maggidim* that fasting and asceticism were essential for *teshuvah*, the Baal Shem Tov taught that sincere dedication of oneself to the will of G-d was the essence of *teshuvah*.

The Baal Shem Tov's inspiring spirit was like water for a parched throat, and Chassidus soon attracted a large following. Although Shabbetai Zevi was no longer on the scene, Shabbetean groups continued to function under the leadership of self-proclaimed prophets. Coming so soon after the Shabbetai Zevi debacle, some of leading Torah authorities feared that this populist movement headed by a charismatic leader who was a kabbalist might be a repetition of a Messianic movement, and they came out with fierce opposition to and even excommunication of *chassidim*. But there was no stopping Chassidus, which had a meteoric rise in Russia and Poland.

Zeide R' Motele was both a physical and spiritual descendant of the Baal Shem Tov. The Baal Shem Tov's greatest emphasis was on *ahavas Yisrael* (love for a fellow Jew). When he was asked how one can acquire love for G-d, since G-d is so abstract and not subject to perception by any of our senses, the Baal Shem Tov said, "Love your fellow man and that will bring you to love for G-d." The Baal Shem Tov's love for people was unconditional and non-discriminatory. Indeed, he glorified the unlearned Jew who, in spite of virtually intolerable living conditions, maintained a sincere and unwavering faith and loyalty to the G-d of Abraham, Isaac and Jacob.

> The legend regarding the Baal Shem Tov's birth emphasizes the role of unconditional *ahavas Yisrael*. It is related that the Baal Shem Tov's father, R' Eliezer, had an open door for all travelers and was hospitable to all. One Shabbos morning a man knocked on the door, carrying a knapsack and a walking staff and asked for something to eat. R' Eliezer did not reprimand him for violating the Shabbos, but welcomed him and served him all the Shabbos delicacies. The man then said, "I am Elijah, and I came to test you whether you would be hospitable even to a sinner. Your reward for your unconditional kindness is that you will have a son whose *ahavas Yisroel* will be unconditional."

One time the Baal Shem Tov was sharing *seudah shelishis* (the third Shabbos meal) with his disciples and expounding on profound secrets of Torah. In an adjacent room, some of the simple folk were reciting *Tehillim* (*Psalms*). The Maggid of Mezeritch thought, "How fortunate we are to be able to grasp these profound Torah thoughts from the Master, not like those unlearned folk who know nothing more than how to read the *siddur*."

Abruptly, the Baal Shem Tov interrupted his discourse, and asked the disciples to place their arms around their neighbors' shoulders and form a circle. He then put his hands on the shoulders of the disciples beside him. The Maggid relates that he felt he was transported to the highest celestial spheres, where the sweetest strains of the prayers came to his ears. He heard the heart-rending longing, "My G-d, my soul thirsts for You, my flesh pines for You. You are to me like water for a parched throat in the desert" (*Psalms* 63:2). "Create in me a new heart, O G-d, and renew a spirit within me" (*Psalms* 51:12). "Like a hart calls out for streams of water, that is how my soul cries out for You" (*Psalms* 42:2). The tears flowed profusely down the Maggid's face, and he thought, "If only I could reach a spirituality so pure and sincere to be able to call out to G-d like this."

The Baal Shem Tov removed his hands from his disciples, and the wondrous vision stopped. Then he said, "The enchanting strains you heard were those of the simple folk reciting the *Psalms*. Do you not wish you could attain their intensity of devotion to G-d?"

There are many wondrous tales told about the Baal Shem Tov, but the dearest to me are those that demonstrate his love for every Jew. The Baal Shem Tov was able to make the lowliest people feel worthy and important because that is how he truly felt about them.

One Friday night the *chassidim* observed a simple man praying with great joy and fervor. They asked the Baal Shem Tov, "What is it that gives him this intense exaltation?" The Baal Shem Tov said, "Let us follow him and see."

They followed the man to his humble hut, and watched through the window as he greeted his wife with a hearty, "Good Shabbos," and joyfully sang the hymn greeting the angels. They saw that the table was covered with a coarse cloth, and except for two small candles, was bare.

The man said, "My dear wife, please bring me the wine for *kiddush*."

The wife brought two small loaves of challah, upon which he recited the *kiddush*. He took a bite of the challah and said, "What a delicious wine! Fit for a king! Kindly bring me the Shabbos fish."

The wife brought plates of cooked beans for him and herself. The man ate the beans and said, "My dear wife! The fish this week is superb." He sang a Shabbos song and asked for the soup.

Again the wife brought in beans, which he ate and then remarked, "What a delicious nectar!" When he asked for the main course, the wife again served beans. "I have never tasted roast duck as delicious as this," he said.

The Baal Shem Tov said to his disciples, "This man's joy of observing G-d's day of rest is so great, that it enables him to taste gourmet dishes in beans, just as our ancestors in the desert could taste any desired food in the manna."

For me this story is of twofold significance. First, it shows the spiritual level attainable by even the simplest person. Second, where there is true love, beans can be a delicacy. Where there is a lack of true love, the finest gourmet foods can be tasteless.

The Baal Shem Tov's love for every Jew may be characterized by his statement, "I wish that I could have as much love for the greatest *tzaddik* as G-d has for the worst *rasha* (sinner)."

The chassidic masters who followed the Baal Shem Tov all excelled in *ahavas Yisrael*. Stories abound about their care and consideration for others. The following story is just one of many.

R' Levi Yitzchok of Berditchev was fastidious about performing a *bris* (circumscision) first thing in the morning, so as not to delay this great mitzvah. When his grandson was born, his *chassidim* knew that the *bris* would be performed promptly at sunrise, and they were all assembled by that hour. Surprisingly, R' Levi Yitzchok remained in his study. When he failed to appear after several hours, the *chassidim* conducted the morning service without him. Someone peered through the keyhole and saw him in profound mediation. No one dared disturb him.

As the afternoon progressed, his son-in-law knocked on the door, but there was no response. Finally, at four o'clock R' Levi Yitzchok emerged, and the *bris* was performed. When it came to naming the infant, R' Levi Yitzchok declared, "His name in Israel shall be called Moshe Yehudah Leib." His son-in-law was taken by surprise, since it was customary to name a child after a family member, and he could not recall any Moshe Yehudah Leib in the family.

Everyone joined in the *seudah* (festive meal) following the *bris.* R' Levi Yitzchok addressed his son-in-law, "You are no doubt wondering why I was so late for the *bris* and why the name Moshe Yehudah Leib.

"When I awoke this morning, I sensed that a terrible darkness had settled upon the world. I then realized that the *tzaddik* R' Moshe Yehudah Leib of Sasov had died, and that the world had lost the brightness of his being.

"I then heard a voice announcing to all the *tzaddikim* in *Gan Eden* (Paradise), 'Come greet the *tzaddik* R' Moshe Yehudah Leib,' but the latter did not appear. Instead, he had jumped into *Gehinnom* (Hell), and was pacing to and fro. The angels in *Gehinnom* approached him and ordered him to leave and go to his rightful place in *Gan Eden*, but R' Moshe Yehudah Leib refused.

"'I devoted my entire lifetime to rescuing and redeeming Jews who had been imprisoned in dungeons by the *poritzim* (feudal lords). I see many thousands of souls imprisoned here in *Gehinnom*, and I will not leave here until I have liberated them.'

"The angels responded, 'The mitzvah of freeing captives applied only during your stay in the physical world. Now that you have passed on, you are no longer obligated to perform mitzvos."

"R' Moshe Yehudah Leib responded, 'The Almighty knows that I never did mitzvos for the sake of reward. I redeemed my fellow Jews from captivity because of my love for them. I will not be able to partake of the bliss in *Gan Eden* knowing that so many souls are suffering the torment of *Gehinnom*. Either they are released to accompany me to *Gan Eden*, or I remain here to suffer along with them.'

"The angels were perplexed. Never before had that someone willingly entered *Gehinnom* and refused to leave. They sent a message to the Heavenly Tribunal for guidance, and the tribunal ordered that R' Moshe Yehudah Leib must leave *Gehinnom*.

"R' Moshe Yehudah Leib responded, 'All my life I lived according to the word of G-d. I will not leave here except by an express command of G-d. I wish to plead my case before Him.'

"The Heavenly Tribunal agreed and invited R' Moshe Yehudah Leib to appear before the Divine throne. R' Moshe Yehudah Leib refused to budge. "G-d is everywhere,' he said. 'I will plead my case from here.'

"R' Moshe Yehudah Leib then set forth a heart-rending plea. 'We know that the Master of the universe conducts the world *middah keneged middah* (measure for measure). During my lifetime on earth I zealously performed the mitzvah of *pidyon shevuyim* (redeeming the imprisoned). I pray that the Master of the universe invoke His principle of *middah keneged middah* and empower me to redeem the souls confined to *Gehinnom*.'

"G-d decreed that R' Moshe Yehudah Leib's argument was just, and He ordered the angels to review how many people R' Moshe Yehudah Leib had redeemed, and to calculate how many of their offspring, until the end of time, would never have come into the world had they remained in the dungeons for the rest of their lives. The total came to some sixty thousand. G-d then ruled that *middah keneged middah*, R' Moshe Yehudah Leib could take sixty thousand souls out of *Gehinnom*.

"R' Moshe Yehudah Leib went through *Gehinnom*, looking into every nook and cranny for the most forlorn *neshamos* that were least likely to be released, and after gathering them together, he led them into *Gan Eden*.

"I could not tear myself away from observing this great tzaddik's unparalleled *ahavas Yisrael*, and it was only after he had completed his task that I could attend to the *bris*. I gave the child the name of this great *tzaddik*, that he may one day learn about him and follow in his footsteps."

This story exemplifies the intensity of *ahavas Yisrael* of our *tzaddikim*.

Zeide R' Motele used to say, "My *chassidim* think that I am a *tzaddik*. How can I be a *tzaddik* if I feel a greater love for my own children than I do for others? But this much I can tell you. If any one of my *chassidim*, however distant he may be, feels pain even in his little finger, I feel that pain."

In the second generation after the Baal Shem Tov, Chassidus began to stress the importance of cleaving to a *tzaddik*. The opponents of Chassidus sharply criticized this as forming a "*tzaddik* cult," and that people thought that as long as they were followers of a *tzaddik*, the *tzaddik* would serve as their proxy. The *tzaddik* would study Torah and perform the mitzvos properly as their representative, and they did not have to exert themselves in the Divine service. They accused Chassidus of encouraging belief in the *tzaddik* rather than pure belief only in G-d.

This was an unfair indictment. The principle of closeness to a *tzaddik* is proposed by the Talmud. The Torah says that a person should "cleave unto G-d" (*Deuteronomy* 11:22). How can a mere mortal possibly cleave unto G-d? the Talmud asks. The answer is that if one cleaves unto a Torah scholar, it is considered as if he were cleaving unto G-d (ibid. *Rashi*). Chassidus did not at all advocate that the *tzaddik* serve as a proxy. Rather, that he be a model whom his followers should try to emulate in performance of the mitzvos. By their cleaving unto the *tzaddik*, the *tzaddik* is able to elevate people to greater spirituality. Belief in the *tzaddik* is not heresy, as evidenced by the statement in the Torah that when the Israelites witnessed the miracle of the dividing of the Reed Sea, "They believed in G-d and in Moses, His servant" (*Exodus* 14:31).

We have no way of gauging the greatness of the Baal Shem Tov. This was best expressed by his successor, the Maggid of Mezeritch, who said, "I am thrilled whenever I see the Baal Shem Tov's son, R' Zvi, because that is a testimony that he was indeed a human being, a mortal. Otherwise, it would be impossible for me not to think of him as a heavenly angel."

Chapter 4
The Origins of a Tzaddik:
The Czernoble Legacy

Zeide R' Motele's mother died when he was nine. His father, R' Zusia of Tolumutsch, remarried and moved to Galicia. Zeide R' Motele was reared by his mother's father, R' Yaakov Yisroel of Cherkassy, who was a son of the Maggid of Czernoble.

The dynasty of Czernoble began with R' Nochum, who was a disciple of the Baal Shem Tov and later of his successor, the Maggid of Mezeritch. R' Nochum authored the work *Meor Eynaim* (Light of the Eyes), one of the earliest chassidic texts conveying the teachings of the Baal Shem Tov.

R' Nochum could trace his ancestry back through thirty-six generations of Torah scholars.

> One of his ancestors was a simple person of whom R' Nochum was very proud. This ancestor used to produce mead from the honey he bought from peasants. He would never buy more than enough honey to make a three day supply. When his wife told him that he would lose his providers, who would look for better customers for their honey, he said,

"That is not my concern. G-d will provide for me. I am obligated to do something to earn a living, but I am not obligated to think that far ahead."

R' Nochum was an *elui* (child prodigy in Torah), and at a young age studied *Kabbalah*. He was orphaned as a child and was raised by an aunt, who showed preference to her own children, giving Nochum the smallest portion of food. One time his aunt left the house after preparing the meal. Nochum was hungry, so he took the smallest portion, which he knew would be his. When the aunt returned, she beat him. When Nochum said that he had taken the smallest portion, the aunt said, "True, you did not take more than your share. Nevertheless, you should never take even what is yours without asking permission." Many years later, R' Nochum said, "I never forgot that. Even if one is certain he is right, one must always ask."

Upon R' Nochum's arrival, the Baal Shem Tov said to his wife, "Beware of this man. He is a *goniff* (thief)." Observing R' Nochum's great piety, the Baal Shem Tov's wife asked for an explanation. The Baal Shem Tov said, "There is a cluster of *neshamos* in *Gan Eden* which he is plotting to steal for his descendants."

The story of the *tefillin* and the *esrog* is well known, but for the sake of completion I must relate it, as I heard it from my father.

After R' Nochum's death, his rebbetzin would visit his colleagues, who helped support her. She was welcomed with great respect by R' Baruch of Medhzibohz, the Baal Shem Tov's grandson, who said to her, "Tell me some of the practices of your holy husband."

The rebbetzin thought for a few moments, then abruptly arose. "I must leave here," she said. "After the many years we were together, not a single thing comes to my mind. What is worse, I cannot even picture what he looked like. I must take this as a sign that I do not belong here."

R' Baruch escorted her to the coach. Just as the driver was about to depart, she stopped him and emerged from the coach. "I would never have shared this episode, but inasmuch as nothing else came to my mind except for this episode, I take this as a sign that I must tell it.

"My husband had a pair of tefillin that was very dear to him. The parchments had been written by the scribe, R' Ephraim. His stature can be gathered from the Baal Shem Tov's comment that after Ezra Hasofer and Nechemiah Hasofer, R' Ephraim is third in line.

"We lived in great poverty. There was a wealthy man who offered to pay fifty rubles for these tefillin. Fifty rubles! That was a small fortune that we could live off for at least a year or more. I said to my husband, 'Sell the tefillin. For five rubles you can buy a pair of tefillin that meet the most exacting standards, and we will be able to have food and clothing.' But my husband was adamant. The tefillin were not for sale.

"There were times when we had no firewood and no food. I said, 'Where is your feeling for the children who are cold and hungry? Sell the tefillin.' But no, there was no use talking.

"I was raising my orphaned niece, Malkele. I said to my husband, 'When Malkele needs a dowry to get married, will you sell the tefillin?' He yielded to this and said, 'To marry off a child, one may even sell a sefer Torah.' That was my only consolation. The tefillin would provide a dowry for Malkele, so I didn't bother him about it again.

"One Succos there were no esrogim to be had. My husband was very upset that he would not be able to fulfill the mitzvah of esrog and lulav.

"On Erev Succos, he saw someone at a distance carrying an esrog and lulav. He ran to him and asked him how much they would cost. The man said, 'Rabbi, this is not within your means. It is the only esrog in the entire region. This is for the wealthiest person in town, who is paying fifty rubles for it.'

"My husband reasoned, 'I have put on the tefillin today, and I do not need them for the next eight days of the festival. The

esrog I need for a mitzvah now.' He ran home, took the *tefillin* to the rich man and got fifty rubles with which he bought the *esrog* and *lulav*.

"*I had been at the market, trying to stretch the few kopeks I had to put some food on the table for Yom Tov. When I returned, I saw my husband's face radiating with joy. 'What is the simchah with you?' I asked. He was reluctant to tell me, but eventually I forced the truth out of him.*

"*When I heard that he had sold the tefillin, I went into shock. The scenes of years of cold nights and the children going hungry flashed before my eyes. He would not sell the tefillin for them. And now he sold them for what? For a piece of fruit that in eight days will be worthless! And worst of all, Malkele's dowry! How will she be able to marry without a dowry?*

"*I flew into a rage and demanded, 'Where is the esrog?' My husband pointed to the cupboard. In my fury, I took the esrog from the cupboard and dashed it on the ground into smithereens.*

"*My husband turned pale, and tears flowed down his cheeks. Then he said softly, 'I no longer have the tefillin, nor do I have an esrog for the mitzvah on Succos. Satan would want me to become angry with my wife and disturb our shalom bayis and the simchah of Yom Tov. I will not give him that gratification.' "And with that he began singing and dancing to greet the festival of Succos. Chassidim would add that no doubt the heavenly angels danced along with him.*"

I know that many people will feel that R' Nochum was wrong in not selling the *tefillin* to provide for his family. But listen to R' Baruch of Medhzibohz's reaction.

"Rebbetzin," he said, "I can understand why your husband did not sell the *tefillin* to provide for you and the children. I can also understand why he did sell them to procure an *esrog* for Succos. What I cannot grasp is how a human being can restrain himself from not reacting in anger at such a moment in order to preserve *shalom bayis*. That is something that only someone like the *Meor Eynaim* (referring to R' Nochum by the *sefer* he authored), only someone with superhuman *middos*, is capable of."

Incidentally, these *tefillin* were subsequently acquired by Zeide R' Motele, and he made a festive meal in celebration of this acquisition. These precious *tefillin* are a cherished treasure in our family.

My father used to enjoy relating that R' Nochum's son, R' Mordechai, known as the Maggid of Czernoble, said, "Even non-Jews appreciated my father." He related the following.

> My father would go to the *mikvah* before saying the midnight prayers mourning the loss of the Temple. In winter, he would break the ice in the pond to immerse himself. A non-Jewish neighbor could not tolerate seeing him freezing, so he would build a fire alongside the pond for my father to warm up. He would get into a conversation with my father.
>
> "I am very upset with my son," he said. "He is a lout, a drunkard, a lazy bum who refuses to do a stitch of work. I think I have to throw the good-for-nothing out of the house."
>
> "Don't be so harsh on him," my father said. "Look at me. I am a good-for-nothing, too."
>
> "Oh," the man said, "if my son was like you, I'd be satisfied."

"So you see," R' Mordechai said, "even non-Jews appreciated my father."

In their poverty, R' Nochum and his wife shared one old, worn-out coat. When his *chassidim* bought him a coat, R' Nochum refused to accept it. "The only commendable trait I have," he said, "is that I am satisfied with living an austere life, as the Talmud says in *Ethics of the Fathers* (6:4). Do you wish to deprive me of that?"

> After seeing people flock to R' Nochum for his blessings, someone challenged him, "What makes you think that you are qualified to give blessings? Aren't you misleading people to think that you have special powers?"
>
> R' Nochum answered, "The Torah says that prior to going out to war, the *Kohen* (priest) would announce that all those who are newly married, or have not reaped the first fruit of their vineyard, or have not moved into a newly built house or

are afraid that their sins would make them vulnerable to the enemy are all exempt from military service lest they be killed in battle (*Deuteronomy* 20:5-8).

"What was the point of all these exemptions?" R' Nochum asked. "The soldiers were protected from harm by Divine Providence. The only justifiable exemption was the sinful person, whose behavior may have forfeited Divine protection. All the others had no reason to fear being killed in battle.

"However," R' Nochum continued, "if the sinful person would be the only one exempt, then his exemption would constitute a public humiliation, revealing to all that he was a sinner. The Torah sharply condemns public humiliation. Therefore, other exemptions were added, so that the sinful person would not be exposed. It could be assumed that he was exempt for one of the other reasons cited.

"So it is with me," R' Nochum said. "My function is to help people do *teshuvah* and correct their ways. But that would identify anyone who consulted me as being a sinful person who is in need of instructions on *teshuvah*. People would be reluctant to consult me because that would be a public humiliation, a public disclosure that they are sinful.

"In order to allow people to consult me for instructions on *teshuvah*, I also give *berachos*. That way it may be assumed that people are coming to me to get my blessings, and not because they are sinful. Once they come, I can teach those who are in need of guidance for *teshuvah*."

The practice of a *tzaddik* dispensing *berachos* was thus to protect the dignity of the *baal teshuvah*.

R' Nochum was a disciple of the Maggid of Mezeritch, and when the Maggid lectured, R' Nochum stood afar, able to hear every word from a distance. One time, the Maggid was telling his other disciples about R' Nochum's greatness, and R' Nochum drew closer, eventually standing beside the Maggid and cupping his ear. The Maggid said, "When I lecture on Torah, R' Nochum hears from a distance. When I was relating his greatness, he could not hear it, and he thought I must be whispering. That is why he drew close. He is truly humble and has trained his ears not to hear what he did not wish to hear."

R' Nochum had trained not only his ears, but his eyes as well. One Friday night, when he left his study, the lamp extinguished. A non-Jew who was nearby re-lit the lamp. When R' Nochum returned, he groped around, striking his head on the wall. When he was asked what the trouble was, he said that he could not see in the dark. Inasmuch as it was light, no one could understand him. It was then discovered that the lamp had gone out and had been re-lit on Shabbos. R' Nochum's eyes could not see by a light that was kindled on Shabbos, even though it was done by a non-Jew.

> In his travels, R' Nochum came to a town where the mikvah was in disrepair. The only person who had the money to restore the mikvah was a miser. R' Nochum told the man that he would give him his portion in *Gan Eden* if he provided the funds for the mikvah. The miser quickly seized upon the bargain. When *chassidim* asked him how he could divest himself of his portion in *Gan Eden*, R' Nochum said, "We say in the *Shema* that we are to love G-d with all our heart, with all our soul and with all our possessions. How could I ever fulfill that mitzvah when I own nothing? The only thing I owned was my portion in *Gan Eden*, and that was all I had that I could give away for a mitzvah."

R' Nochum set the precedent for his descendants to gather funds to redeem Jews whom the *poritzim* had imprisoned in dungeons. One time, R' Nochum was imprisoned on a trumped-up charge. He was visited by a colleague, R' Zev of Zhitomir, who said, "G-d told Abraham, 'Leave your home and go to the land that I will show you' (*Genesis* 4:1). Abraham had excelled in providing food and drink for weary wayfarers. G-d said, 'What you are doing is indeed commendable, but until you have been a wayfarer yourself, you will not understand their needs.' So it is with you, R' Nochum. You indeed worked to free the imprisoned, but until you experienced the agony of prison yourself, you could not know what it was like. Now that you have had a taste of it, you will increase your efforts."

When R' Nochum came to a community, he would visit the local *shochet* to inspect his knife to see whether the blade was smoothed to perfection. In one community, the *shochet* thought he would smoothen the blade to greater perfection before showing it to R' Nochum. He then reflected, "If someone had brought me a chicken just now, I would have used the knife as it is. If is kosher enough for use, then it is good enough to show to the *tzaddik*." When R' Nochum was given the knife, he returned it to the *shochet* without inspecting it and smiled, saying, "If it is good enough to use for G-d, it is good enough for Nochum."

Chapter 5
R' Mordechai, the Maggid of Czernoble

R' Mordechai was probably the first to use the name Twersky. (All our relatives spell it this way. My father came to America from Poland, where he spelled his name "Twerski").

It is unclear how the name originated. There is a town in Russia "Tver." "Tversky" would then mean "from Tver." However, I have never heard that any of our ancestors had any connection to Tver.

A distant relative, R' Sender Yerushalimsky, said that his ancestor and the Maggid were close friends. When they were told to choose a surname, they decided to choose cities in Eretz Yisroel. Sender's ancestor chose Jerusalem, hence their surname is Yerushalimsky. The Maggid chose Tiberias (Teveryah), hence our surname, Tversky (or Twersky).

> Chassidic lore relates that the Maggid of Mezeritch told his disciples that a special *neshamah*, which had not been in this world for centuries, was destined to come down. R' Nochum went to the *tzaddik*, R' Pinchas of Koretz, to pray for him that

he acquire this special *neshamah.* "Come with me to the mik-vah," R' Pinchas said.

After immersing in the mikveh, R' Pinchas said to R' Nochum, "You will have this *neshamah.*" R' Nochum said, "I want generations of *tzaddikim.*" R' Pinchas immersed again and said, "You will have that." "I want my descendants not to be dependent on others," R' Nochum said. R' Pinchas responded, "That I cannot do for you. But people will be dependent on them, and they will be dependent on people."

After R' Nochum left, R' Shneur Zalman came to Koretz with the same request. "You came too late," R' Pinchas said. "R' Nochum already succeeded in acquiring the special *ne-shamah.*" That year R' Mordechai was born.

As was noted, R' Nochum lived very sparsely.

As a child, R' Mordechai accompanied his father on his travels and asked, "Is it appropriate to appear before people in worn-out clothes which bespeak your poverty?" R' Nochum said, "When I come to people who are oppressed and deprived, I wish to identify with them. Furthermore, life is full of tempta-tions, and the best way to resist them is to live in austerity."

The young Mordechai responded, "But, Father, one can ban-ish much darkness with just a bit of light. The hearts of the deprived and oppressed can be uplifted when they see their leaders as princes rather than as paupers."

R' Mordechai indeed lived more comfortably. When R' Nochum visited his son, he scented the aroma of fish. In astonishment he asked his son, "It is not Shabbos. How come you have fish in the mid-dle of the week?"

A *chassid* who had been a follower of R' Nochum had the *chutzpah* to say to R' Mordechai, "Why are you deviating from your father's life style? He traveled with a horse that could barely pull the wagon, but you travel with a chariot."

R' Mordechai smiled and said, "You can buy a live chicken for just a few kopecks, but if an artist sculpts the likeness of a chicken, it can be expensive. My father was a real *tzaddik*, so he came cheap. I am but an imitation of him, so I come more dear."

The esteem in which R' Mordechai was held by other *tzaddikim* is evident from a comment made by the *tzaddik*, R' Moshe Zvi of Savran. "I cannot understand why people go to R' Mordechai of Czernoble with petitions to pray for them. Whereas the Talmud says that if a person has a sick family member he should ask a *tzaddik* to pray for him (*Bava Basra* 116a), it also says that we may not petition angels for help. R' Mordechai is an angel, who has been assuming a human disguise for years."

R' Ahron of Karlin, one of the Mezeritch Maggid's major disciples, died very young, leaving a daughter, Sarah. The Maggid told R' Nochum to visit R' Ahron's grave and tell him that Sarah should be the wife of R' Mordechai.

At the assemblage of the young couple's engagement, R' Menachem Mendl of Vitebsk was honored with reading the *tenaim* (articles of engagement). It is customary when the father of the bride or groom is deceased, to cite someone else who "gives them away." R' Mendl read the *tenaim* aloud, and when he came to, "Standing at the side of his daughter, the *kallah* (bride), is R' Ahron," he fainted. When he was revived, the Maggid asked him, "Why did you faint? Don't you know our R' Ahron (who had died several years earlier)?" R' Mendl said, "I did not realize that in such a short life span one could achieve such radiance." The Maggid said, "You are a *battlan* (ne'r-do-well). Why, Levi Yitzchok (of Berditchev) sees much more than you, but he does not faint."

R' Mordechai's wife died young, and he took as his second wife the daughter of R' Dovid Leikus, a disciple of the Baal Shem Tov. R' Dovid was always of a joyous demeanor, even though he was beset by many tragedies, losing his wife and several children. His demeanor did not change even when he was sitting *shivah*. "The Baal Shem Tov says that G-d does nothing bad. It is just that with our human perception we cannot see the good." The townsfolk who knew his disposition avoided the usual platitudes of consolation. However, two people who came from afar were not aware of this, and they said the usual adages, "What is man, and what is his life?" "Man is like a broken potsherd, like a dream that vanishes," etc. In order to placate them, R' Dovid acted as if in grief. But when they continued their litany, he was no longer able to tolerate it. "Listen here," he said, "a human being is very dear, more precious than heavenly angels. Wherever he is, in this world or the next, the Divine light shines over him. There is no agony, no evil, no travail, only Divine goodness. We must obey the rituals of mourning as prescribed by the Shulchan Aruch, but with true faith in G-d's infinite benevolence, we need not feel sad."

R' Mordechai (often referred to as "the Czernoble Maggid") had eight sons, all of whom became chassidic masters and established dynasties. His eldest son and successor was R' Ahron. R' Yaakov Yisroel of Cherkassy, whom we refer to as "the Cherkassy Zeide," was the third of the eight sons. R' Mordechai once said, "My sons are like the seven candles of the Menorah." Someone remarked, "But you have eight sons." R' Mordechai responded, "Do you think that a father is unaware of how many children he has? The Torah says that the High Priest, Ahron, kindled the seven lights of the Menorah. My son, Ahron, does the same."

One time, R' Mordechai took R' Ahron along with him on a journey. They were given adjacent rooms at an inn. At night, R' Ahron heard some conversation going on outdoors. He parted the curtains and saw his father conversing with the occupant of a coach. R' Mordechai had one foot on the running board, and when the coach started moving, he hopped alongside it.

In the morning the Czernoble Maggid asked R' Ahron, "Did you see anything last night?" R' Ahron told him what he saw.

"The man in the coach wished to be Mashiach. I did not approve of him. We have waited so long for Mashiach, that we deserve something better."

The money R' Mordechai received from his *chassidim* was dispensed for *tzedakah*, especially to redeem Jews who had been imprisoned by *poritzim*. It was also known among *chassidim* that R'

Mordechai knew the identities of the thirty-six concealed *tzaddikim* (*Succah* 45b) and that he supported them clandestinely. Stories about R' Mordechai's awareness of the hidden *tzaddikim* abound.

In a village near Berditchev there lived a pious Jew who had a spice store. One time he came to Berditchev to buy merchandise, and was met by the *tzaddik*, R' Leib, son of Sarah. R' Leib said to him, "Young man, what are you doing here?" When he said he was there to buy spices, R' Leib said, "Lend me the money you have for three months."

The merchant was reluctant to give away the money he needed to buy merchandise, but R' Leib was obviously a *tzaddik*, and he could not refuse him. "Do you have any spices in the store?" R' Leib asked.

"Just a small amount," the merchant said.

"Good," R' Leib said. "Go back and sell it."

The merchant was able to borrow money to procure more merchandise. Toward the end of three months, a customer bought some spices and left, leaving behind his purse in the store. The merchant ran after him to return the purse, but was unable to find him. He put the purse away, expecting its owner to retrieve it.

On his way to shul, the merchant met R' Leib, who said, "Did you receive the money I borrowed from you?" Upon returning home, he opened the purse and found the exact amount he had lent R' Leib.

The merchant hurried back to the shul and told R' Leib that the money had been returned. "The money you lent me was used to redeem a Jew from the dungeons. You had a great mitzvah. Ask for a reward and you will receive it."

The merchant was no fool and exploited the opportunity. "I want to meet one of the thirty-six hidden *tzaddikim*," he said.

"A difficult request," R' Leib said, "but I must keep my word. You must travel to this village and go to the local tailor. He is one of the hidden *tzaddikim*. Take along a torn garment and ask him to repair it for you."

The merchant did as he was told. Approaching the tailor's humble shop, he saw there was a handsome chariot standing there. Upon entering the shop, he saw the tailor engaged in a conversation with a person of stunning appearance.

"What do you want?" the tailor asked.

The merchant showed him the torn garment, which the tailor deftly repaired. The merchant put a ruble on the table.

"The work I did is worth only a few kopecks," the tailor said. "A ruble is far too much."

The merchant said, "I am on a journey and I need this garment. To me the job you did is worth a ruble," but the tailor was reluctant to accept it.

The other man in the shop spoke up, "If he says that to him your work is worth a ruble, then you may take it."

The merchant returned to R' Leib and related the incident. R' Leib said, "Do you know who the other man in the shop was? That was R' Mordechai of Czernoble. He travels among the thirty-six hidden *tzaddikim* to support them."

In Poland, a contemporary of R' Mordechai was R' Dovid of Lelov. R' Yitzchak of Vorki was a disciple of R' Dovid, and after the latter's death, he visited various *tzaddikim* to find a Rebbe. Accompanied by R' Dovid's son, R' Moshe, he came to Czernoble. When they introduced themselves as coming from Poland, the Maggid asked them, "Did you perhaps know the *tzaddik*, R' Dovid of Lelov?" R' Yitzchak said that he was a disciple of R' Dovid, and that his friend was R' Dovid's son.

The Maggid said, "My father (R' Nochum) would come to me in a dream every night. Abruptly, I did not see him for forty days. I did much soul-searching to discover what I had done wrong to lose this privilege.

"After forty days, my father again appeared and told me that R' Dovid of Lelov had died and had entered *Gan Eden*, where he had expounded on the secrets of Torah for forty consecutive days. 'I could not tear myself away to come to you,' he said."

Chapter 6
The Cherkassy Zeide —
R' Yaakov Yisroel of Cherkassy

T he Cherkassy Zeide was very assertive, even as a child. One time, when the Baal Shem Tov's grandson, R' Baruch of Medhzibohz, came to Czernoble, R' Mordechai sent his *chassidim* to greet the *tzaddik*. Yaakov Yisroel was a young boy, and joined the throngs of *chassidim* who greeted R' Baruch. All the *chassidim* stretched out their hands to give *Sholom Aleichem* (a welcoming greeting) to the *tzaddik*, and little Yaakov Yisroel pushed his hand through the crowd. When R' Baruch took the child's hand, he pulled him from amidst the crowd. "Who are you?" he asked.

"I am a son of the Czernoble Maggid," the child said.

"And who says that your father is the Czernoble Maggid?" R' Baruch asked.

"The same one who says that you are the Rebbe R' Baruch," the child answered.

R' Baruch later said to R' Mordechai, "Your little son really put me in my place."

The Cherkassy Zeide was an outstanding Talmudic scholar. His encyclopedic knowledge of Talmud earned him the appellation of "my library" from his father. Before R' Mordechai died, he gave each of his sons an assignment. To the Cherkassy Zeide he said, "You are a great *lamdan* (Torah scholar). You should become a *melamed*." In order to fulfill his father's wishes, the Cherkassy Zeide taught Talmud to three people: his younger brother, R' Dovid of Talna, R' Naftali Halberstam, son of the rebbe of Shinuvi, who had married his granddaughter, and the Zeide R' Motele.

Zeide R' Motele's Torah scholarship is legendary, and he was well aware of the outstanding Torah knowledge of his father-in-law, the *tzaddik* of Sanz. But he once confided to my grandfather, his son, R' Leibele, that "The Zeide (of Cherkassy) surpassed my father-in-law in Talmudic genius. However, he beswore us never to reveal anything of his Talmudic knowledge." Why the Cherkassy Zeide concealed his immense Torah knowledge is a mystery.

Although the Cherkassy Zeide did not permit any disclosure of his Talmudic erudition, there were many manuscripts of his discourses on Chassidus. Unfortunately, these were destroyed in the fire that consumed Zeide R' Motele's library in Hornosteipol. A small remnant remains in *Emek Tefillah* (Valley of Prayer. The word *emek* can also mean "profound," and indeed, the essays are on the proper concentration in prayer). He cites verses from the Torah and elaborates upon them, saying, "From this we can derive a teaching in the Divine service," or "We must understand this verse in the light of *mussar.*"

The Czernoble children were very supportive of the Kollel R' Meir Baal Haness of Ukraine, a fund to provide sustenance for Jews in Israel. There was a *nasi* (president) of the Kollel, and this was considered a position of great honor. R' Ahron and the Cherkassy Zeide competed for the position of *nasi*, which seemed to result in a rift between the two brothers.

That this was not a petty ego dispute is evident from the following story.

> One time, R' Ahron came to Cherkassy. The *chassidim* were in a quandary what to do. Should they go to greet him? Perhaps the Cherkassy Rebbe would be offended, since the two brothers were apparently adversaries. Should they not go to greet

him? That would be snubbing a son of the Czernoble Maggid. They, therefore, did not venture out of their homes.

After R' Ahron left, the Cherkassy Zeide asked his *chassidim*, "Did you greet my brother?" They replied that they were afraid the Rebbe would be offended.

"Offended?" the Cherkassy Zeide said. "Foolish people! The angels in heaven would wish to understand the nature of the dispute between my brother and me. How dare you accuse us of personal interests?"

(Incidentally, the last *nasi* of the Kollel was Zeide R' Leibele. We have the document, a colorful poster, designating him as the *nasi*).

The Cherkassy Zeide used to give *kameyos* (amulets). Normally, Shalosh Seudos extended late into the night. One Shabbos the Zeide hurried through *shalosh seudos*, and as soon as it was permissible, told his gabbai (assistant) to take a swift horse and go to this particular village to a certain person's house and make sure he has his *kamaye*. Upon arriving at this house, he found that the man had already left. He was a dealer in lumber, and had traveled off to the woods. He had indeed forgotten the *kamaye*. The wife found it, and the gabbai took it and ran to find him.

On entering the woods he found that a tree had fallen upon the man. The *kamaye* was later opened, and it read:

"I order you, trees of the forest, not to kill this man.

Yaakov Yisroel B'harav (son of the rabbi)."

One time, while en route by boat from Cherkassy to Hornosteipel accompanied by a number of his *chassidim* for the wedding of Zeide R' Motele's daughter, the Cherkassy Zeide abruptly turned to them and asked, "Does any remember so and so?" Several of them responded, "Yes, he died several years ago." The *chassidim* hear him mumble to himself, "So he couldn't get to me anywhere else but on the river." The *chassidim* were overcome with awe, that the rebbe was being confronted with a *neshamah* that needed *tikkun* (rectification).

The Cherkassy Zeide said to them, "He was a fine person, right?" The *chassidim* responded, "Of course! He was one of us."

Toward dawn, they arrived at their destination, where horses and wagons were waiting to transport the crowd. Each *baal agalah* (wagon driver) was hoping to take the rebbe, who chose a coach harnessed to two horses.

As they traveled, the Cherkassy Zeide said to the *baal agalah,* "I want a favor from you."

"Anything the rebbe wants is my wish," the latter answered.

"I want you to give me that horse as a gift," the rebbe said, pointing to one of the two horses.

The *baal agalah* was taken aback by this strange request. This was his favorite horse, the one that could pull him out of any swamp. Giving up that horse could ruin his livelihood.

"Let me stop off at your house to rest up a bit," the Cherkassy Zeide said.

While in the house, the Cherkassy Zeide got into a conversation about the deceased person of whom he had inquired from his *chassidim*. The *baal agalah* said, "We were partners. I had loaned him some money which he never repaid."

"Do you still have the note on that loan?" the rebbe asked. At the rebbe's request, the *baal agalah* searched through his papers and found the note. "Can you give me this note as a gift?" the rebbe asked. When the *baal agalah* consented, the Cherkassy Zeide tore up the note.

Soon afterward, someone came in and told the *baal agalah* that his favorite horse had suddenly died. When the Cherkassy Zeide saw his anguish, he said, "Because he had been in debt to you when he died, his *neshamah* was reincarnated as a horse to work off the debt. Now that the debt was cancelled, his *neshamah* can be at peace. And because you gave me the gift of the note that made possible the release of his *neshamah*, I bless you with long life."

Uncle Nochum said that some of Zeide R' Motele's *chassidim* remembered this man, who lived to be one hundred and eight.

Among the Czernobler children the *minhag* (custom) was to have *hagba'ah* (lifting the Torah) at *Minchah* on Shabbos.

The Cherkassy Zeide used to put on his glasses by *hagba'ah*.

He explained, "I used to be able to see from one end of the world to the other. But this was interfering with my *avodah* (Divine service), so I asked that it be taken from me, except for once during the week, Shabbos *Minchah* by *hagba'ah*. So I put on my glasses in order that I should see better."

As a young man, the Cherkassy Zeide once lodged at an inn. When the innkeeper found out that his guest was a son of the Czernoble Maggid, he said, "I have a special room for you." He unlocked a drawer and took out a little box which contained a key. He led him to a room which he unlocked, and showed him a high bed. "You can rest here," he said.

"No sooner did I lie down on the bed," the Cherkassy Zeide said, "than I began trembling severely. Like the Patriarch Jacob, I felt 'How awesome is this place. This is surely a G-dly place and this is the gate to heaven' (*Genesis* 28:17).

"I went down to the innkeeper. 'What is the story of this bed?' I asked. He told me that the Baal Shem Tov had slept there. Upon hearing this, I went back up on the bed and had the most wonderful sleep of my life."

When a grandson was born, the Cherkassy Zeide recited the prayer in which the child was given a name. When he came to the phrase, "And his name in Israel shall be called," he paused for several moments, then said, "Mordechai Dov Ber" (this was a cousin to Zeide R' Motele). He later explained his pause.

"My first thought was to name the child Mordechai, after my father. Last night I dreamt of my father-in-law, the Mittler Rebbe, R' Dov Ber, so I added that name. But just as I was about to pronounce the name, R' Levi Yitzchok of Berditchev appeared (he had died several decades earlier). I paused to think, is it proper to give a child such an extensive name, Mordechai Dov Ber Levi Yitzchok? Then I realized that the reason R' Levi Yitzchok had come was as a *mechuten* (relative by marriage) and not because he wanted his name added." Years later, R' Mordechai Dov Ber indeed married into R' Levi Yitzchok's family.

This story is particularly dear to me because it is essentially a first person story.

I met an elderly cousin who was a grandson of the rebbe of Koidanov. He told me that when he was a child of nine, he had a *melamed* (tutor) who was not a *chassid* of his grandfather. "Why are you not a *chassid* of my grandfather?" he asked.

The *melamed* said, "I was a *chassid* of your great-great-grandfather, the rebbe of Cherkassy. The practice was that at *shalosh seudos* (the third Shabbos meal), the rebbe would expound on Torah until it was dark. When Shabbos was over, he would have someone light candles and he would continue his Torah discourse until late.

"This one Shabbos, the rebbe did not expound on Torah. He was deep into meditation. No one brought in candles, and we sat silently in the dark.

"All at once, the rebbe opened his eyes and said, 'The Talmud says that on Shabbos, all the *neshamos* (souls) that are in *Gehinnom* (Hell) are released. When Shabbos is over, there is a declaration, "The wicked must return to Hell" (*Psalms* 9:18). But how can this be? We have a principle not to make a declaration of punishment.'

"We all sat silently, not knowing what to answer. Then the rebbe said, 'I'll tell you the answer. There is a place known as *avadon* (lost), in which souls are doomed to eternity. But I say that souls should be released even from *avadon*. Do you all agree?'

"We all responded, 'Yes, we agree.'

" 'Then let someone bring in candles,' the rebbe said.

"When the candles were brought in, we saw that the rebbe was in a cheerful mood. He said, 'The declaration "The wicked must return to Hell" is not a declaration of punishment at all. To the contrary, it is a declaration that the *neshamos* that had been doomed for eternity in *avadon* may be released to *Gehinnom*, from which they will be released after twelve months.'

"And so," my *melamed* said, "if I was a *chassid* of a rebbe who could release doomed *neshamos* from *avadon*, can you expect me to be a *chassid* of anyone else?"

We will refer to the Cherkassy Zeide and the Czernoble legacy numerous times. Let us now go on to another aspect of Zeide R' Motele's *yichus*.

Chapter 7
The Origins of a *Tzaddik*:
The Chabad Legacy

The Cherkassy Zeide married Devorah Leah, daughter of R' Dov Ber, a son of the Alter Rebbe. R' Dov Ber was known as the Mittler Rebbe.

The story revolving around this match is most fascinating. The Alter Rebbe heard from the great Maggid of Mezeritch that Mashiach would be born of the descendants of his oldest disciple and the youngest. The Alter Rebbe calculated that R' Nochum of Czernoble was the oldest disciple, and that he himself was the youngest. He set off to Czernoble to research the possibility of finding a mate for his granddaughter, Devorah Leah. Upon arriving in Czernoble, he informed R' Nochum about the nature of his visit. R' Nochum told him that he did not have any young children, but that his son, R' Mordechai, had several young boys.

Together they visited R' Mordechai, who took the Alter Rebbe into the room where the boys were sleeping. The Alter Rebbe placed his hand upon each boy's forehead. Upon reaching the young Yaakov Yisroel, the Alter Rebbe said, "This one has a warm forehead. He is mine. Do not try to substitute another child for him, because I will recognize him immediately." The *shidduch* was promptly sealed with a L'Chaim.

When R' Baruch of Medzhibozh visited R' Mordechai of Czernoble, he, too, said that he wanted to have one of the latter's sons as a husband for his daughter. R' Mordechai showed him where the children were sleeping. "Go in and choose," he said.

R' Baruch put his hand on each boy's forehead. When he felt the young Yaakov Yisroel's forehead, he said, "Ah! A warm head! This one is for me."

R' Mordechai shook his head. "You're too late," he said, "the Litvak already took him." (The Alter Rebbe was affectionately referred to as "the Litvak" because he resided in Liadi in Lithuania).

At the Cherkassy Zeide's wedding, R' Mordechai, in wishing L'Chaim to the guests, blessed them that G-d may bestow upon them "spiritual and physical blessings." The Alter Rebbe, on the other hand, blessed them with "physical and spiritual blessings."

R' Mordechai said to the Alter Rebbe, "*Mechuten!* You give priority to physical over spiritual blessings?" To which the Alter Rebbe responded, "The Patriarch Jacob first asked G-d for 'bread to eat and clothes to wear,' physical blessings, and only afterward 'and G-d will be a G-d to me,' spiritual blessings" (*Genesis* 28:20).

R' Mordechai responded, "Yes, but what was physical to the Patriarch Jacob is far superior to what is spiritual for us."

The Cherkassy Zeide was sixteen when he married Devorah Leah, and was fortunate to spend two years under the tutelage of the Alter Rebbe in Liadi. We have only a few stories about their relationship.

The Alter Rebbe said to his newly acquired grandson, "Now that you are in our family, you will include the verse *ki bonu bocharto* in the Friday night *kiddush*. (This verse was omitted by the rebbes of Czernoble.)"

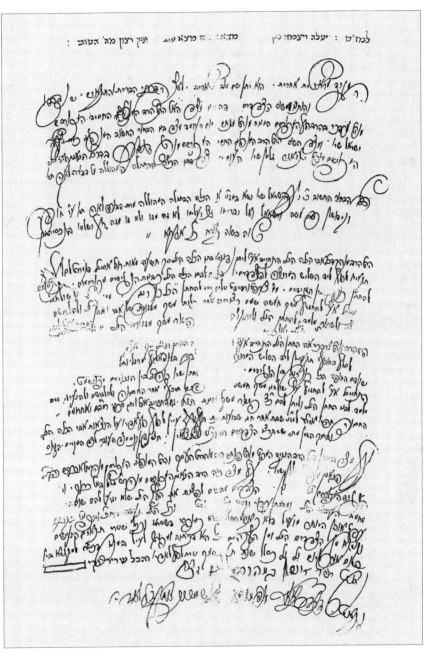

Tenaim (engagement contract) of the Cherkassy Zeide, which cites R' Mordechai,
son of R' Menachem Nochum (Meor Eynaim), father of the choson, R' Yaakov Yisroel,
and R' Dov Ber, son of R' Shneur Zalman, father of the kallah.

Chapter Seven: The Origins of a Tzaddik: The Chabad Legacy / 69

The young Yaakov Yisroel was very assertive and responded to the sage, "If grandfather will say *veshomru* Friday
night, I will say *ki bonu bocharto*. (The practice of Chabad is to
omit *veshomru*, because it is considered an interruption between the *Shema* and the *Amidah*.)"

The Alter Rebbe stroked his beard and said, "This beard is
too white for me to take on any new practices. However, when
my *siddur* will be printed, I will have *veshomru* included."

This is why *veshomru* appears in the Chabad *siddur*, although it is
not recited by Chabad *chassidim*.

Prior to Zeide R' Motele becoming rebbe, he went to his great-uncle,
R' Ahron of Czernoble, for *semichah* (ordination). It was customary for
all Czernobler descendants to receive *semichah* from one of the senior
Czernobler rebbes. R' Ahron gave him *semichah*, but stipulated that he
must retain the practice of Czernoble, and stop saying *ki bonu bocharto*
in *kiddush*.

Incidentally, Zeide R' Motele did not say *ki bonu bocharto* except on
two occassions: the first Shabbos when he became Rebbe in
Hornosteipol, and forty years later, on the last Shabbos of his life.

Another interesting exchange occurred when the Alter Rebbe
told his grandson that he wanted him to listen to a Chassidus
discourse. He sat the Cherkassy Zeide at his immediate right,
and expounded on a Chassidus theme. When he finished, he
said to him, "Now, review what I said."

"I didn't hear it," the young grandson said.

"But you were sitting right here," the Alter Rebbe said.

"I do not hear what I have no permission from my father to
hear," the grandson said.

The Alter Rebbe did not take any offense at this. Rather, he said
to the young grandson, "I want you to go back to your father
and ask his permission to hear my discourses on Chassidus."

We must understand something about *avodas Hashem* (service of
G-d). We might best grasp this by an analogy to an army. There may
be several generals, each one in charge of a particular region. Each one
has a particular strategy which his subordinates are compelled to

observe. It is a serious offense for one officer to decide on his own that he wishes to adopt the strategy employed by another general. One may not deviate from one's assignment.

Our *tzaddikim* knew exactly what it was that they were meant to accomplish in the world. There are a number of ways of implementing Torah and mitzvos, all of which are holy. Each *tzaddik* knew precisely in which way he was to serve Hashem, and was not free to deviate. The Cherkassy Zeide had received his *derech* (method) of *avodas Hashem* from his father. Although the *derech* of the Alter Rebbe was equally true and holy, he felt that he was not free to accept it.

It is written that each of the twelve tribes had its own unique way of performing the Divine service. All were equally holy, but one did not overstep the boundaries. Similarly, although the Cherkassy Zeide knew that the Alter Rebbe's way was true and holy, he did not feel at liberty to deviate from his father's version without his approval.

There is a letter from Zeide R' Motele to my great-uncle, R' Boruch Dovid'l, in which he says that the holy Alter Rebbe made a very careful edition of the *siddur*, but nevertheless, "You should not change from the version we have been using."

The Cherkassy Zeide did indeed ask and receive permission from his father. It is of interest that the few remaining Torah discourses that survived the fire that destroyed Zeide R' Motele's library resemble the style of the Alter Rebbe rather than that of the Czernobler Chassidus in the *Meor Eynaim*. Zeide R' Motele's Chassidus writings also bear a heavy imprint of Chabad. In one letter he writes to Zeide R' Leibele, telling him to study the *Tanya* from cover to cover. When R' Levi Yitzchok of Berditchev first saw *Tanya*, which is a small book, he said, "What a wondrous thing R' Shneur Zalman did! He took an infinitely great G-d and put Him into such a little book."

The Chassidus of Chabad has a unique flavor. It is more philosophical and contemplative than other schools of Chassidus.

In *Kabbalah* there is frequent reference to the ten *sefiros*. In *Kabbalah*, G-d is generally referred to as *Ein-Sof* (inifinite) and the *sefiros* are emanations of *Ein-Sof.*

Kabbalah explains that G-dliness is so overwhelming that nothing, not even heavenly angels, could exist in the immanent presence of G-d. Inasmuch as G-d wished there to be a universe with both spiritual and physical components, He emitted radiations which, though of Divine origin, were attenuated and veiled so that there could be a creation. This may be thought of as similar to looking at the sun through a smoked glass. It is impossible for the human eye to look directly into the brightness of the sun without being severely damaged, but if the darkness of the glass dims the brightness of the sun's rays, one may be able to look at the sun.

The ten *sefiros* are divided into the cognitive and the affective. (The translations of the kabbalistic terms leaves much to be desired, but we will do the best we can.) The first three *sefiros*, *chochmah* (data), *binah* (understanding) and *daas* (knowledge) are cognitive. *Chochmah* is data, the raw material out of which *binah* forms concepts. *Daas* organizes concepts and transmits them to the affective *sefiros*.

There are seven affective or "emotive" *sefiros*: *chesed* (loving-kindness), *gevura* (strength), *tiferes* (splendor), *netzach* (triumph), *hod* (glory), *yesod* (foundation) and *malchus* (majesty). The human intellect and affects correspond to the ten *sefiros*.

The *sefiros* underwent progressive degrees of attenuation and veiling, ultimately reaching a level wherein the Divine light is so concealed that the denial of its existence is feasible.

At the risk of oversimplification, most chassidic schools emphasized the seven affective *sefiros*, concentrating on how a person should channel the energies of these emotions to the service of G-d. Chabad, in contrast, emphasized the three cognitive *sefiros*. (Chabad is an acronym for **Ch**ochmah, **B**inah, **D**aas.) This emphasis resulted in philosophic speculation, which some of the Alter Rebbe's contemporaries felt was hazardous for the average person, who might distort some of these sensitive concepts and endanger pure *emunah* (faith).

The Alter Rebbe's premise is that intellect can dominate and control emotion. The Talmud says that a person does not commit a sin unless he is overcome by a spirit of folly (*Sotah* 3a). The folly that can result in sin is the failure to value an intimate relationship with G-d and that sin is an obstacle to such a relationship. If a person's cognition was intact and he was aware that sin can sever his relationship to G-d, he would not deviate from the Divine will.

The Alter Rebbe also posited that within every Jew there is love for G-d, but that it is obscured by the many temptations to which a human being is subject. Every person is capable of having an intense love for G-d if one would eliminate the inhibiting factors that prevent this love from being expressed.

Tanya elaborates on the *nefesh Elokis* (Divine spirit) and the *nefesh behamis* (animal spirit) that comprise the spiritual component of a human being. The Alter Rebbe said, "As a youngster I reflected on these two spirits within man. I concluded that the *nefesh Elokis* is anchored in the will that the understanding of the intellect, the emotional drives, thought, word and deed should all be directed toward the study of Torah, the performance of mitzvos and the refinement of character traits.

"The *nefesh behamis,* even though it too is spiritual, arouses the intellect and emotions, and I recognized that the *nefesh Elokis* pursues truth, whereas the *nefesh behamis* is false in essence and seduces a person with a variety of falsehoods.

"I searched for a method that would enable me to identify any thought or feeling, whether it derived from the *nefesh Elokis* or the *nefesh behamis.* When G-d enlightened me to realize that a person's intellect is capable of recognizing the truth of the *nefesh Elokis* and the falseness of the *nefesh behamis,* I knew that I had arrived at the true path in life."

These themes, developed in the Alter Rebbe's youth, permeate the philosophy of Chabad.

Several of the Alter Rebbe's colleagues criticized him for teaching to the laity lofty concepts of G-dliness that are beyond their ability to understand. The Alter Rebbe responded with a parable.

> A king had a beloved son who fell seriously ill. The doctors could not find a cure, and he was close to death. One doctor said that there is one remedy: pulverizing a particular precious stone and having the prince drink it. The only jewel of this kind was in the king's crown. The king promptly ordered that it be crushed and administered to the prince.
>
> The prince was moribund and could not drink the preparation. With difficulty they opened his mouth and were able to get in a few drops of the solution. Most of the liquid containing the priceless jewel fell to the ground, but enough was absorbed by the prince to enable him to recover.
>
> "So it is with the lofty concepts of G-dliness," the Alter Rebbe said. "Most of these teachings may fall to the ground, but even if just a few tiny drops enter people's minds and hearts, it can elevate them spiritually."

In relating stories about Zeide R' Motele's forebears, my point is to cite those characteristics which help mold his character and his spirituality. Stories about the Alter Rebbe abound.

> The Alter Rebbe was the youngest disciple of the Maggid of Mezeritch and was especially dear to him, as evidenced by the fact that he assigned his son, R' Avraham the *Malach* (angel) to study both the revealed and esoteric Torah with him. The Alter Rebbe said, "We agreed that he would teach me *Kaballah* for three hours. When the *Malach* was not looking, I set the clock back, and maximized my time with him."

> The Alter Rebbe's colleagues distinguished him by giving him the title of "Rav." One time the Maggid told R' Zusia, "Write to our gaon to come." When the Alter Rebbe heard how the Maggid had referred to him, he took this as indicative of a distancing and fainted. When the Maggid heard of this, he said, "I had no idea that he was so sensitive. I was like a son to the Baal Shem Tov, and Zalman is like a son to me."

The following story indicates his understanding of and perspective on Torah.

> The Alter Rebbe used to be the *baal koreh* (reader of the Torah) on Shabbos. After his death, the first time his son heard the reading of the *Tochachah*, citing all the horrible punishments that would befall Israel if it deviated from the Torah, he fainted. When he was revived he explained that he had never heard such terrible tidings before. "When my father read the *Tochachah*, one heard only blessings, not curses."

As mentioned, the Talmud requires that a person thank G-d for the bad as for the good. "No evil emanates from the Most High"

(*Lamentations* 3:38). We are unable to see the hidden good in bad things that happen. R' Zusia's and the Alter Rebbe's faith superceded their human perception.

During the lifetime of the Maggid of Mezeritch, there were no harsh anti-Semitic decrees, but these recurred after his death. Some of his disciples wondered, "Inasmuch as the Talmud says that *tzaddikim* are even greater after their death than in their lifetime (*Chullin* 7b), why does the Rebbe not exercise his powers in Heaven to forestall these decrees?" The Maggid appeared to them in a dream and said, "When I was alive and with my mortal vision perceived something as bad, I prayed to annul it. From my perspective here I can see the good that will ultimately emerge from it. I cannot intercede to annul a good."

It was this kind of perspective that forged the character of Zeide R' Motele.

After the Alter Rebbe's death, the Cherkassy Zeide lived with his father-in-law, R' Dov Ber (Mittler Rebbe). Under his father-in-law's tutelage he continued his advancement in both halachah and *Kabbalah*. It was said of the Mittler Rebbe that if you opened one of his veins, it would be Chassidus rather than blood that would flow.

R' Dov Ber married off his daughter to the son of R' Levi Yitzchok of Berditchev. At the wedding, R' Levi Yitzchok asked R' Dov Ber to deliver a Torah discourse, but R' Dov Ber refused. R' Levi Yitzchok then asked the Alter Rebbe to intervene. R' Dov Ber said, "I cannot say Torah in the presence of R' Levi Yitzchok, because he goes into so passionate a fervor that it will confuse my thoughts." R' Levi Yitzchok assured R' Dov Ber that he would not do so.

No sooner did R' Dov Ber begin his Torah discourse than R' Levi Yitzchok began to gesticulate so violently that the table shook, spilling the wine and causing the goblets to break.

When R' Levi Yitzchok was reminded of his promise, he said, "What could I do? When R' Dov Ber began speaking words of Torah, the heavenly angels descended and began dancing joyfully to the sweetness of his words. But I feared that the angels might be jealous that a mortal has so superceded them, and might try to harm him. I acted in a way to frighten away the angels."

As was noted, the Cherkassy Zeide concealed his Talmudic erudition, revealing it only to the three students. This was also true of the Mittler Rebbe.

How many of us have been able to figure out just what, exactly, is our *tafkid* (mission) on earth? These *tzaddikim* knew exactly what it was they were supposed to do.

There were many geonim (outstanding Talmudic scholars) who were well versed in *Kabbalah*, but did not teach nor write about *Kabbalah*. Conversely, there were many *tzaddikim* who were geonim, but kept their Talmudic erudition concealed.

R' Menachem Mendl of Lubavitch's (Tzemach Tzedek) enormous halachic erudition is evident from his voluminous and virtually incomparable responsa. His father-in-law, the Mittler Rebbe, left works on Chassidus, but nothing on Talmud. When a halachah question came to the Mittler Rebbe, he would give it to the Tzemach Tzedek to answer. The Mittler Rebbe, would review the answer, and never corrected it.

> One time a question came when the Mittler Rebbe was away. The Tzemach Tzedek, knowing that the question would be given to him, responded. When the Mittler Rebbe returned and saw the answer he had written, he pointed out to the Tzemach Tzedek that he had overlooked the opinion of one *rishon* (early Talmudic commentary). The Tzemach Tzedek was very upset by this. The Mittler Rebbe consoled him, "Never mind. You are not a rebbe yet."

The Mittler Rebbe had a photographic memory. In the Alter Rebbe's library there was a book on *Kabbalah*, on which the Alter Rebbe had written that it is prohibited to study it. During a fire in the library, this book was lost, and the Alter Rebbe was saddened by this loss. He asked his son whether he perhaps remembered its contents. The Mittler Rebbe said,

"How could I, when it was prohibited to study it?" The Alter Rebbe remarked, "And you did not have *mesiras nefesh* to learn some additional concepts of Chassidus?"

The Mittler Rebbe wrote prolifically. When he wrote the last line of a page, the ink of the first line was still moist.

> One time, the Mittler Rebbe was deep in thought, and he did not hear his infant crying. The Alter Rebbe, who lived in the apartment above, came down and picked up the child. The Mittler Rebbe was oblivious to all of this, and his father reprimanded him. "Meditation in Torah should never render you oblivious to someone's cry."

On the ninth day of Kislev, 5524 (1834), the Mittler Rebbe was delivering a chassidic discourse on the verse: "A recollection of Your abundant goodness they will utter" (*Psalms* 145:7). When he recited the verse, "The source of life is with You," (*Psalms* 36 :10) he returned his soul to its source. He was fifty-four years of age.

Upon the Mittler Rebbe's death, the Cherkassy Zeide returned to Czernoble, but the seventeen-year absence and his adoption of Chabad Chassidus resulted in his feeling estranged from his brothers. With his father's consent, he settled in Hornosteipol. Many of his father's *chassidim* followed him, and his father would even tell some *chassidim*, "Go to my son, Yaakov Yisroel."

Hornosteipol became a hub of Chassidus, where the Cherkassy Zeide held court for twenty-seven years. Abruptly, he announced that he was moving to Cherkassy and gave no reason for this. The *chassidim* pleaded with him not to leave, and an eyewitness gave this account.

"Everybody in Hornosteipol, men, women and children, escorted the Rebbe. Their wailing could be heard from a distance. The non-Jewish population, seeing the profound expression of grief, wept along with them. We walked behind the Rebbe's coach until the river edge. When the Rebbe alighted from the coach, he turned to the people, his face radiating. 'I promise you,' he said, 'that Hornosteipol will not be put to shame.' We did not understand this at the time."

Three years later, Zeide R' Motele became Rebbe in Hornosteipol.

Chapter 8
The Origins of a *Tzaddik*:
The Karlin Legacy

R'Ahron of Karlin is known as "the great R' Ahron." Whereas all the disciples of the Maggid of Mezeritch excelled in all *middos*, the Maggid once said that Chassidus is based on the love of G-d, the love of Torah and the love of Israel, and that three of his disciples are outstanding in these *middos*: R'Ahron in the love of G-d, R' Shneur Zalman in the love of Torah and R' Levi Yitzchok in the love of Israel.

R' Ahron was introduced to Chassidus by his uncle, R' Menele, of whom we know little. Our sole knowledge of R' Menele is a comment which may be seen as the all-encompassing principle of the Karlin contribution to Chassidus. R' Menele cited the prayer in the Shabbos morning service: "By the mouths of the just You are exalted, by the lips of the righteous You are blessed, by the tongues of the pious You are hallowed and amidst the holy You are praised." This is followed by "In the assembly of the multitudes of Your People, the House of Israel, Your Name, our King, is praised in song." R' Menele commented, "It says that G-d is exalted by the just, but it does not say 'by Menele.' He is blessed by the righteous, but it does not say 'by

Menele.' He is hallowed amidst the pious, but it does not say 'by Menele.' He is praised by the holy, but it does not say 'by Menele.' But when it says that 'the multitudes of the House of Israel praise G-d in song,' Ah! Menele is among the multitudes."

R' Menele totally effaced himself as an individual, and saw himself worthy of serving G-d only in conjunction with the greater household of Israel. Standing alone, a person who is neither just, righteous, pious or holy cannot approach G-d. If a person considers himself as possessing any one of these traits, he is vain, and vanity distances one from G-d. A person's salvation can be only in his joining himself with other Jews, because the prophet says, "Your nation, as a whole, are righteous" (*Isaiah* 60:21). The shortcomings of an individual disappear when he effaces himself and is just one member of the greater unit, the Jewish People.

> A poor widow complained to R' Ahron that she had made a *shidduch* (matrimonial match) for her daughter, but that if she does not deliver a dowry, the *shidduch* will be broken. R' Ahron gave her money for the dowry. Several weeks later she again approached him, this time crying that she had no money to buy her daughter a wedding gown. R' Ahron gave her money for a gown.
>
> R' Ahron's wife was upset by this. "I can understand why you gave her the money for the dowry in order to save the *shidduch*, but why did you have to give her additional money for a gown? That was not necessary to save the *shidduch*. You could have given that money to other needy people."
>
> R' Ahron responded, "That idea occurred to me, too. Then I reflected, if this is the counsel of my *yetzer tov* (good inclination), then why did it not urge me to give this money to the needy before the widow came? I could only conclude that this was the counsel of my *yetzer hara*, and I refused to listen to it."

R' Ahron used to recite *Shir HaShirim* (Song of Songs) on Friday with great devotion. The Maggid of Mezeritch said that the heavenly angels were envious of R' Ahron's devotion in *Shir HaShirim*. One time R' Ahron was chanting *Shir Hashirim* softly in his own quarters.

The Maggid sent a messenger to tell him to cease saying *Shir HaShirim*, because "you are creating such a commotion in heaven that it disturbs my rest." *Chassidim* would say that there is nothing remarkable about R' Ahron's recitation of *Shir HaShirim* causing commotion in heaven. There is also nothing remarkable in the fact that the Maggid could sense this. What *is* remarkable is that the Maggid's accomplishment with his rest superceded what R' Ahron accomplished with his *Shir HaShirim*.

R' Ahron's devotion in prayer was so intense that it caused R' Shneur Zalman to say, "R' Ahron's soul departs from him during prayer, and he is virtually resurrected after praying."

> Shortly before Passover, R' Ahron told the Maggid that he wished to be with his family for the festival. The Maggid wished him a safe trip. No sooner had he left, than the Maggid sent several of his disciples to bring him back. "The Rebbe called for me?" R' Ahron said. The Maggid responded, "Have a safe trip." After R' Ahron left, the Maggid again sent people to bring him back. This occurred three times, after which R' Ahron left for home.
>
> Several days later, R' Ahron died. His colleagues then understood that the Maggid's repeatedly calling him back was in order to keep him at his side, which would have prolonged his life, but they had not realized this. Inasmuch as R' Ahron was very dear to them, they complained to the Maggid why he had not explicitly told them to prevent his leaving. "We would have put him in chains to keep him here."
>
> The Maggid responded, "I could not be explicit. The Torah says that G-d said of Moses that 'he is trustworthy in My entire household' (*Numbers* 12:7). What is meant by 'trustworthy in My household?' There wasn't anything in heaven that Moses could steal. Trustworthy means that Moses could be trusted to keep a secret. Sometimes one is entrusted with information that one may not reveal."

R' Ahron was only thirty-six when he died.

We do not have many of R' Ahron's teachings. His son, R' Asher and his grandson, the second R' Ahron, were Chassidic masters in their own right, and the latter's work, *Beis Ahron*, conveys many of his grandfather's teachings.

R' Ahron formulated an important principle of Chassidus in his statement, "There is nothing in Torah that indicates that it is a mitzvah for men to immerse in the mikvah. However, there is nothing as conducive to performance of mitzvos as immersion in the mikvah. There is nothing in Torah that indicates that sadness is a sin. However, there is nothing as conducive to sin as dejection."

One great bequest is *Kah Echsof*, the beautiful Shabbos song for which he composed both the words and the meditative melody. It is sung by many *chassidim* on Friday night. Just this single composition is enough to tell us of R' Ahron's intense love of G-d, Israel, and Shabbos.

G-d, I long for the sweetness of the Shabbos, which becomes the twin and is united with Your treasured nation. Extend the sweetness of Your reverence to the nation that seeks Your favor. Hallow them with the Shabbos' holiness which unites itself with Your Torah. Grant them sweetness and desire to open the gates of Your will.

You Who were and are — protect those who observe and anxiously await Your holy Shabbos. As the hart entreats by springs of water, so their soul entreats to gain the sweetness of the Shabbos that is united with Your holy Name. Spare the ones who delay leavetaking from the Shabbos, that it not be sealed off from them in the six days that absorb sanctity from the holy Shabbos, and purify their hearts with truth and faith to serve You.

May Your mercy overwhelm Your attributes, and may Your mercy overflow upon Your holy nation, to water those thirsting for Your kindness, from the river flowing forth from Eden, to crown Israel with splendor — those who glorify You through Your holy Shabbos, to endow them all six days with the heritage of Jacob, your choicest one.

The Shabbos! — sweetness of souls. The Seventh Day! — delight of spirits and bliss of souls, to be blissful with Your love and awe. Holy Shabbos! — my soul pines for your love. Holy Shabbos! — the souls of Israel find refuge in the protection of your wings. They are sated from the abundance of Your house.

Chapter 9
The Origins of a *Tzaddik*: The Sanz and *Baruch Taam* Legacy

Although Zeide R' Motele's emergence as a *tzaddik* of stature was well-developed before he married the daughter of R' Chaim Halberstam, the *tzaddik* of Sanz, there is no doubt that his father-in-law was very influential.

R' Chaim's father, R' Leib Halberstadt, was not a *chassid*. At age ten, R' Chaim heard of the Seer of Lublin, and he persuaded his father to take him to Lublin. The Seer embraced young Chaim'l and said to his father, "This child is going to become one of the great Torah leaders of his generation." R' Chaim became a disciple of the Seer.

> When still very young, the outstanding Torah scholar, R' Baruch Frankel, known for his Talmudic commentaries and halachic responsa, *Baruch Taam*, chose R' Chaim as a husband for his daughter, Rochel Feige. Shortly before the wedding, the young woman found out that R' Chaim had a severe limp, and she refused to go to the *chuppah*. R' Chaim asked to have a few words with her in private, and she agreed to speak with him.

Although no one was privy to their conversation, the story circulates that R' Chaim asked his *kallah* to look into the mirror. When she did so, she saw herself with a severe deformity. He then told her that she had been destined to be deformed, but since she was his *basherte* (predestined mate), he had intervened, spared her of the pain and took her deformity upon himself. Needless to say, Rochel Feige consented to marrry him.

R' Baruch used to say, "My son-in-law may have a weak leg, but he has a very strong mind."

R' Baruch was extremely proud of his son-in-law. One time, he hosted the great gaon R' Yaakov of Lisa, author of *Nesivos Hamishpat*. R' Yaakov complained that he did not see anyone who was capable of being the Torah authority of the next generation. R' Baruch pointed at his son-in-law and said, "We can rely on him." R' Yaakov then entered into a Talmudic discussion with the young R' Chaim, then concurred, "Yes, we can rely on him."

R' Baruch also exchanged responsa with the outstanding Torah scholars, R' Mordechai Benet of Nikolsburg and R' Moshe Schreiber (*Chasam Sofer*). Many editions of the Talmud contain commentaries by R' Baruch.

R' Baruch's *ahavas Yisrael* was legendary. One time he heard his daughter conversing with the household help and laughing. He reprimanded her, "Don't you know that Mordechai who tends the bathhouse is sick in bed? How can you engage in mirth when someone is suffering?"

In his later years, R' Baruch lost his vision. Rather than being saddened by this, he was actually pleased. He said that his loss of vision occurred because he had often strained his eyes by studying Torah by a dim light. He said, "The Talmud says that Torah will be perpetuated only if one risks his life over it (*Berachos* 63b). Inasmuch as I sacrificed my vision for Torah, I am confident that Torah will be perpetuated in my descendants."

In his earlier years, R' Baruch was opposed to the chassidic movement, believing that *chassidim* neglected Torah study.

When his son, R' Yehoshua Heschel, became a follower of the Seer of Lublin, R' Baruch told him that he was not welcome at home.

After several years, R' Yehoshua Heschel longed to see his father. He returned home and sat outside the room where R' Baruch was lecturing. He overheard the discussion of a thorny problem for which no solution was found. During the break, he called aside one of the students and told him to suggest a way to resolve the difficulty. When the class resumed and the student offered the explanation, R' Baruch realized that this brilliant solution was beyond the ken of this student. "Who told you this explanation?" he asked. The student said that it was the young man in the outer chamber. R' Yehoshua Heschel was invited in, and son and father were happily reunited.

One time the Seer told R' Yehosuah Heschel that he should visit R' Azriel Horowitz, who was the outstanding Torah scholar in Lublin, and was a fierce opponent of chassidism. One time, R' Yehoshua Heschel overheard the proceedings in a *din Torah* (litigation) in R' Azriel's *beis din* (rabbinic tribunal). Two of the judges argued opposing positions, and R' Yehoshua Heschel was astonished that R' Azriel was supporting the wrong argument.

R' Yehoshua Heschel did not wish to be disrespectful by contradicting R' Azriel. Instead, he asked R' Azriel to help him understand a particularly complex Tosafos. In the process of doing so, R' Azriel realized that the position he was supporting was incorrect. The following day, R' Yehoshua Heschel asked the secretary about the verdict, and was thrilled to learn that R' Azriel had reversed himself.

The next time R' Yehosha Heschel was at the Seer, the latter told him, "There is no reason for you to go to R' Azriel any more. You have fulfilled your purpose there."

Interestingly enough, although R' Baruch gained great respect for the scholarship of his son and son-in-law, he personally remained aloof from other *chassidim*.

The *tzaddik* of Sanz, often referred to as the "Divrei Chaim" (the title of his halachic and chassidic works), was famous for his boundless *tzeddakah*. He was eulogized by his son, R' Yechezkel of Shinuvi, who said, "My father was a great Talmudic scholar, but there were other Talmudic scholars as great as him. He was zealous in his service to G-d, but there were others who equaled him. His *tzeddakah* was phenomenal, but there were others who equaled his *tzeddakah*. But that all three traits should come together in such great quality and quantity as with my father, in that he was unique."

Zeide R' Motele, too, was lavish in giving *tzeddakah*. On one occasion, when a *chassid* complained that he was in dire straits, Zeide R' Motele had no money to give him. He removed the silver buttons from his *beketsche* (robe) and gave them to the *chassid* saying, "You can exchange these for money."

My great-grandmother, Babba Raitza, often complained that she did not have enough money for the household expenses. One time she saw a wealthy *chassid* leaving the study, and she knew that he had given Zeide R' Motele a handsome donation. She immediately asked him for some money for the household expenses, but he said he had none to give her.

"That cannot be," she said. "I'm sure that this *chassid* must have given you money."

"Indeed he did," Zeide R' Motele replied, "but that money is not mine. You see, I have two pockets in my vest. One is for me, and the other is for *tzeddakah*. That money went into the *tzeddakah* pocket, and I cannot use it for our personal needs."

Babba Raitza was not satisfied with this. Zeide R' Motele then said, "For reasons known only to Him, G-d has given some people wealth, while others are poor. He has appointed agents to make a more equitable distribution. I am one such agent, and I receive a small wage for this function. If I take more than is my due, that would be embezzlement, and G-d has no use for agents who embezzle."

Babba Reize was still not satisfied with his explanation. Zeide R' Motele then said, "I married you because of your father's reputation. He is most renowned for his *tzeddakah*. If you do not consider that a commendable trait, then what *yichus* do you have?'

Babba Raitza had no response to that.

The *tzeddakah* of *hachnosas kallah* (providing funds to enable people to marry) was especially dear to Zeide R' Motele.

> One time a man complained that his daughter's wedding date was imminent and that he could not provide the dowry he promised. Zeide R' Motele told him to tell his *mechuten* that he will gurantee the dowry. However, the *mechuten* was not satisfied with a guarantee, and refused to go on with the wedding unless the dowry was remitted. Zeide R' Motele pawned his silver Chanukah menorah to provide for the dowry.

> Every Friday by noon, Zeide R' Motele had the Shabbos candles prepared, and all work in his household was completed well ahead of sunset. One erev Shabbos he delayed until shortly before sunset, because one of the regular *tzeddakah* recipients had not come for his stipend. Since Shabbos was fast approaching, Zeide R' Motele went to the man's home. He found that the man was ill and could not come. He delivered the *tzeddakah* to him.

We are fortunate in having much first hand information about the *tzaddik* of Sanz (d. 1876). I knew several people who knew him, and my father and mother knew many more.

The *tzaddik* had an attendant known as "the tall Raphael," who was constantly in his presence. He conveyed some of his observations of the *tzaddik*. Raphael would play the drums at wedding celebrations, and the *tzaddik* blessed him that he would play the drums at all the *tzaddik's* grandchildren's weddings. When my father and mother were married, Raphael was over one hundred years old, and still played the drums well! Raphael lived several more years after that. He died after the last of the *tzaddik's* grandchildren was married.

There are many wondrous tales about *tzaddikim*, and it is not my intention to relate all of these stories. However, the following story is one that I heard in 1947 from R' Kasriel, a nonagenarian who knew the *tzaddik* of Sanz.

The *tzaddik* of Sanz was given the honor of performing a marriage ceremony. He was given the cup of wine, but closed his eyes and was meditating. The family and guests waited impatiently for the *tzaddik* to begin the *berachos.* Abruptly, he set down the cup of wine and called the bride's parents aside.

"Did all of your children survive?" he asked them. The parents said that they had lost one infant, who was swept away when a river overflowed.

"Can you recall whether this child had any unusual birthmarks?" the *tzaddik* asked.

The bride's mother said, "Yes, he had a mole in the shape of an hourglass on his left shoulder."

The *tzaddik* then had the bride's father take the groom aside, and examination revealed the mole on his left shoulder.

The *tzaddik* asked the groom's parents, "Is this really your own child?" They responded that they had found him as an abandoned infant and had raised him as their own.

"The bride and groom are brother and sister," the *tzaddik* declared. The joyous celebration continued, not as a wedding, but as a reunion with a child they had thought to have died.

This remarkable story of the *tzaddik's* prophetic powers spread rapidly through Galicia. The *tzaddik* of Sanz dismissed this as nonsense. "I have no prophetic powers," he said. "When I saw that I could not get the words of the *berachos* out of my mouth, I knew that something was amiss. I could not imagine what was wrong, except that for some reason, this marriage was not to take place. I could only guess what might be wrong, and I just happened to guess correctly."

There is an interesting story about how the *tzaddik* of Sanz chose a husband for his daughter.

The *tzaddik* had heard about the Talmudic prodigy, R' Avraham of Sochachow, who was a follower of R' Mendl of Kotzk. He interviewed R' Avraham as a prospective son-in-law. He was impressed by the young R' Avraham's erudition, and said to the young man, "If you will become my son-in-law, you will leave Kotzk." (The *tzaddik* of Sanz, as well as several other chassidic leaders, disapproved of the school of Kotzk.) Young Avraham responded, "If you become my father-in-law, I will take you to Kotzk with me." This was a smattering of chutzpah toward the *tzaddik* of Sanz. Nevertheless, he asked for a second interview. R' Avraham agreed subject to the condition that he have the option to test the *tzaddik*'s Talmudic knowledge.

The young prodigy explained, "The reason one tests a prospective son-in-law is because the Talmud says that if one marries off a daughter to a boor it is as if he threw her to the lions (*Pesachim* 49b). By the same token, the Talmud also says that a person 'should even sell all his belongings to acquire the daughter of a scholar as a wife' (ibid. 49a). Then why does one not test the scholarship of a prospective father-in-law? The reason is that one believes that when the father-in-law was chosen for marriage, *his* father-in-law tested him. Well, if the *tzaddik* does not believe that his testing me once is sufficient, then I do not have to rely on the one time he had been tested."

This response was sharp and witty, but nevertheless audacious. The *shidduch* did not materialize.

R' Avraham is known throughout the Torah world as an outstanding Talmudist, as his classical works, *Avnei Nezer* testify. It is obvious that the Zeide R' Motele met all of the *tzaddik* of Sanz's criteria for a son-in-law.

My father said that R' Avraham harbored a resentment toward the *tzaddik* of Sanz for rejecting him. One time R' Avraham said, "When the Gaon of Vilna came to the Eternal World, he was found free of any blemish, except that he had participated with the *misnagdim* (adversaries of the *chassidim*) in their persecution of *chassidim*. The heavenly tribunal ruled that he must accept a punishment. He was given the option of passing by the entrance to *Gehinnom* on the way to *Gan Eden*, or coming back to earth as a *chassid*. The Gaon chose the latter. He was reborn as not only a *chassid*, but as a Rebbe, and not only as just a Rebbe, but as a Rebbe superior to all other Rebbes, yet he remained the same *misnaged*. I am referring to the *tzaddik* of Sanz." R' Avraham was referring to the fact that the *tzaddik* of Sanz adopted many practices of the *ashkenaz* version of the services, which was the mode of the *misnagdim*, rather than the *sefard* version which was used by *chassidim*.

> The *tzaddik* of Sanz's *tzeddakah* is legendary. When his daughter asked for money to buy shoes, he said he had nothing to give her. Shortly afterward, a girl from a poor family asked him for money for shoes, and he gave it to her. The *tzaddik*'s daughter said tearfully, "Why is she better than me?" The *tzaddik* replied, "Anyone will be glad to look after your needs. You are the rabbi's daughter. But who will be concerned with the needs of this poor girl if not me?"

A widow supported herself by selling fruit. Once she complained that she had bought a supply of apples, but someone spread a rumor that her apples were spoiled and she had no customers.

"How could anyone cast aspersions on your merchandise?" the *tzaddik* said. "Let me see the apples."

The *tzaddik* went over to her fruit stall and called out, "Apples for sale! The finest apples in town! Come buy the best apples!"

The townfolk, seeing the *tzaddik* selling apples, quickly bought the entire supply.

"See," the *tzaddik* said, "there was nothing wrong with your apples."

One time, the *tzaddik* looked out the window and motioned to a person to come in. "Suppose you found a purse with money. Would you keep it or try to find its rightful owner?"

"Of course I would try to find its owner," the man said.

"You are a simpleton," the *tzaddik* said. He then called another person and posed the same question. The second man said, "I would keep it." The *tzaddik* said, "You are a scoundrel."

The *tzaddik* then posed the same question to a third person. This man responded, "Rabbi, if I find a purse, only then will I know what I will do. Perhaps I will be able to subdue my *yetzer hara* and return it. Hopefully, G-d will help me withstand the temptation. But until I am placed in that particular position, I cannot predict what I would do."

"You are talking sensibly," the *tzaddik* said.

Raphael, the *tzaddik*'s aide, related that before the *tzaddik* went to sleep, he would tell him to prepare coffee. By the time the coffee was finished, he could hear the *tzaddik* saying *Modeh Ani* and reprimanding himself. "Chaim! What is it with you? You are sleeping away your life."

The *tzaddik* denied that he was depriving himself of essential sleep. He said, "Some people are very fast runners, and can cover a distance in a few moments that would take others much longer. I am a fast sleeper. I can achieve in a few moments of sleep what it takes others hours to do."

(From what we now know about levels of sleep, this can be explained scientifically. There is a level of sleep known as REM (Rapid Eye Movement). It usually requires a long period of other phases of sleep before one has a few moments of REM sleep. If it were possible to control our brain waves to immediately go into the REM phase, we might be able to get along with much less sleep. This may actually be attainable today with biofeedback training. It is perfectly possible that the *tzaddik* of Sanz was able to do this on his own, and get the necessary amount of essential sleep in a brief period of time.)

Zeide R' Motele used to relate the following stories about his father-in-law.

> R' Eliezer of Dzikov, who was a *mechuten* (his son's father-in-law) of the *tzaddik* of Sanz, was once very ill, and the *tzaddik* visited him. When he entered the sick-room, he found the family at the bedside. R' Eliezer was sighing deeply.
>
> The *tzaddik* said, "*Mechuten*! What is all the sighing for? You know that it is no more than a transition as from one house to another, or taking off one garment and putting on another."
>
> R' Elizer pointed to his family. "But I must provide for them," he said.
>
> The *tzaddik* of Sanz said, "No need to worry, *Mechuten*. I will provide for them. I will be a father to them and care for them like for my own."
>
> "But, Sanzer Rov," R' Eliezer said, "we are soon to have Rosh Hashanah and Yom Kippur. I serve as *chazan* (reader), and you know that when I sing *Ein kitzva lishnosecha* (There is no limit to Your years), the heavenly angels join in song and clap along with me."

The *tzaddik* of Sanz became very contemplative. "In that case," he said, "have someone warm the mikvah."

The *tzaddik* remained in the mikvah for four hours. Upon emerging from the mikvah, he appeared exhausted but in good spirits. He said, "We can keep him with us."

R' Eliezer lived for an additional thirteen years.

On another occasion, Zeide R' Motele said, "Wondrous happenings were common in Sanz. My father-in-law's reputation as a *wunder-rabiner* (miracle-working rabbi) spread far and wide. Even people remote from Torah observance came for his blessing." He related the following incident.

One day, a Jew from Vienna came to Sanz. He appeared to know little about Yiddishkeit and spoke only German. He said that he was involved in a serious legal process, and although he was totally in the right, the judge did not behave kindly toward Jews, and he was afraid that the judgment would go against him. The *tzaddik* gave him his blessing that he should succeed.

The man appeared puzzled. "I was certain that the Rabiner would draft a petition to the Herr Gott in my behalf. I would like to review the petition to make sure that all the facts are correct."

The *tzaddik* smiled. "No," he said, "the petition is very private. No one may see it."

The man was satisfied. It stood to reason that a petition to "the Herr Gott" must remain secret. "How much do I owe the Rabiner?" he asked. The *tzaddik* told him that there was no charge.

"But I do not wish to burden the Rabiner without compensation," the man said. "It will certainly take much time to write the petition, and I must compensate the Rabiner for his time and effort."

"Very well," the *tzaddik* said. "When you receive a favorable judgment, you may send me three hundred gulden for *tzeddakah*."

A short time afterward the *tzaddik* received a wire transmission of three hundred gulden with an expression of gratitude.

One of the *tzaddik*'s faithful *chassidim* complained, "I have been pleading with the Rebbe for several weeks for relief from my agonizing problem, with no result. Yet, this stranger from Vienna, who is far from Yiddishkeit, has his request fulfilled immediately. Why is he more deserving than me?"

The *tzaddik* replied, "Do you think that wondrous acts are wrought simply? In order to alter any natural process, one places oneself and all one's loved ones in jeopardy. This man was a non-believer, and in order to demonstrate to him that there is a G-d Who is in charge of the world, I was willing to make that sacrifice. Do I have to prove to you, too, that there is a G-d Who runs the world?"

While it is impossible to give even a smattering of the *tzaddik* of Sanz's enormous Torah erudition, I would like to cite just a few nuggets.

The Talmud cites the comment of Jethro when he heard of the miraculous exodus of the Israelites from Egypt. "Jethro said, 'Blessed is G-d, Who has rescued you from the hand of Egypt and from the hand of Pharaoh' " (Exodus 18:10). The Talmud chides Moses and the Israelites for not having said, "Blessed is G-d" for their salvation (Sanhedrin 94a).

The tzaddik of Sanz defended Moses and the Israelites. He cites the halachah which requires a berachah (blessing) when one recovers from a serious illness or is saved from peril. The Ateres Zekeinim rules that even if the patient is no longer in danger, he should wait with reciting the blessing until he has fully recovered (Orach Chaim 219).

Inasmuch as G-d had promised the Israelites that after deliverance from Egypt He would bring them to the Promised Land (Exodus 6:8), they postponed reciting the blessing until their salvation was complete. Rather than being at fault, the tzaddik of Sanz said that it is to the credit of the Israelites that they did not recite the blessing prematurely. They had such

*great faith in the Divine promise that their entry to the
Promised Land was imminent, that they delayed the blessing
until the Divine promise was completely fulfilled.*

As did many other Torah commentaries, the *tzaddik* of Sanz
pointed out that the Torah is not a history text, and that when it
relates past events, it is because they contain a message.

> *He cited the verse in Genesis (18:4) in which Abraham received
> the three angels who appeared as humans, saying to them,
> "Take some water and wash your feet, and lean under the tree."
> In addition to teaching hospitality, there is a homiletic interpre-
> tation to this verse which makes it applicable in all ages.*
>
> *Three of the words in the verse have additional meanings. The
> Talmud says that mayim (water) is symbolic of Torah (Bava
> Kama 17a), and a tree is symbolic of a tzaddik (Psalms 1:3).
> The word regel (leg) also means "habit." The homiletic interpre-
> tation, therefore, is, "Take some Torah and cleanse yourself from
> your habits. If this is difficult for you, depend on a tzaddik to
> help you."*

Someone challenged the *tzaddik* of Sanz for his lavish dispensing of *tzeddakah*, citing the Talmudic edict that one should
not give away more than a fifth of his assets for *tzeddakah*
(*Kesubos* 50a). The *tzaddik* explained, "Every mitzvah has its
regulations. The quantity of matzah that must be eaten to fulfill the mitzvah of matzah is the size of an olive. The length of
the *tzitzis* (fringes) on the *talis* is specified. So, too, the quantity of donations to fulfill the mitzvah of *tzeddakah* has an
upper limit of one fifth.

"However, there is another aspect to *tzeddakah*. The
prophet said that with *tzeddakah* one can redeem oneself
from one's sins (*Daniel* 4:24). Would not a person give away
all he owns to save his life? I must give *tzeddakah* not only as
a mitzvah, but to redeem myself and gain forgiveness for my
many sins."

Chapter 10
The Youth of a *Tzaddik*

At a very tender age, Zeide R' Motele was more than just an accomplished Talmudic scholar, as indicated by the following story.

Zeide R' Motele was a child prodigy in Talmud, and his *gemara melamed* (Talmud instructor) told the Cherkassy Zeide that he could no longer teach the child, because he required a teacher of much greater erudition. A new *melamed* was found, who quickly realized the child's genius. (The *melamed* was R' Shneur Zalman of Trilis, an accomplished Torah scholar, who, at the Cherkassy Zeide's request, left the rabbinate of Trilis to become Zeide R' Motele's *melamed*.)

As noted, Zeide R' Motele's mother died when he was six. At age ten, he told his *melamed* that he wished to complete a volume of the Talmud for his mother's *yahrzeit* (anniversary of the day she died). Just several days before the *yahrzeit* the young Motele had not yet begun a volume, and when he subsequently told his *melamed* that he had completed tractate *Succah*, the latter was in disbelief. "You probably just read the words without really studying it," he said.

Young Motele felt slighted by this remark. "If the rebbe doesn't believe me, let him test me," he said.

"Alright," the rebbe said. "How many times is the name 'Rava' mentioned in *Succah*?"

Young Motele thought a few minutes, then said, "Fifty-two." The *melamed* checked this, and when he found it to be correct, promptly went to the Cherkassy Zeide and resigned his post. "He does not need me as a teacher," he said.

Zeide R' Motele was a frail child, and the Cherkassy Zeide was very vigilant with regard to his health. He assigned a young man, Raphael, who was several years older, to be his *chaver* (study partner) and to supervise his health. The two became bosom friends.

One night, Raphael awoke and saw his young charge sitting on the floor, weeping as he recited the midnight lamentations for the destruction of the Temple. Only toward dawn did Zeide R' Motele return to his bed. Raphael told him that he should not deprive himself of sleep, and when the young Motele continued the practice, Raphael said that he had no choice but to report this to the Cherkassy Zeide, because otherwise he would be derelict in his assignment. Zeide R' Motele pleaded with him not to expose him, to which Raphael responded, "If you promise to take me as your gabbai (aide) when you become a Rebbe, I will keep your secret."

"What makes you think I will be a Rebbe?" young Motele said. Raphael responded, "I know you will."

Years later, when Zeide R' Motele became a Rebbe, he kept his promise and took Raphael as his gabbai. Raphael never revealed these proceedings until after Zeide R' Motele's death.

When Zeide R' Motele was ten, he once disappeared. Everyone in the house went to search for him. Knowing how concerned the

Cherkassy Zeide was about him, they tried to insure that he would not discover that the child was missing. Noticing the tumult, the Cherkassy Zeide asked what was going on, and they had to tell him that Motele was missing. The Cherkassy Zeide joined the search, and eventually they found him hiding under a staircase with a volume on *Kabbalah*. The Cherkassy Zeide took the book from him. "When it is time for you to learn Kaballah, I will teach you," he said.

At age nine or ten an incident occurred which foretold Zeide R' Motele's greatness as a *tzaddik* whose prayers were effective.

> The Cherkassy Zeide was out of town when a man came pleading for the Rebbe's help. He was the proprietor of a small inn in which he himself resided. His inn was a frequent stop-off for poor wayfarers, for whom he provided food and lodging gratis. As a result, he had fallen behind in payment of the rent. The *poritz* who owned the inn sent his hirelings to remove the windows, leaving his wife and children shivering in the bitter cold. The *poritz* threatened to throw him into the dungeon if he did not come up with the money promptly, and he had no prospects of getting the needed sum. He told his tale of woe to the Rebbetzin, who said, "Go into the Beis Midrash, where you will find my grandson, Motele, studying. Ask him to help you."
>
> The man did as he was told, and poured out his misery to the youngster. Zeide R' Motele sighed. "If my zeide were here, he would surely help you, but what can I do for you?'
>
> "But the Rebbetzin sent me to you. I know you can help me," the man wept.
>
> When Zeide R' Motele shook his head sadly, the man arose and said, "If you really are unable to help me, than I bear you no grudge. But if you can help me and you refuse to do so, I will never forgive you, neither in this world nor in the World to Come."
>
> Upon hearing these words, Zeide R' Motele turned pale. He said to the man, "Get a lantern and follow me to the mikvah."

Zeide R' Motele immersed in the mikvah while the man stood, watching. A few moments passed, longer than a person can hold his breath under water, but Zeide R' Motele did not emerge. As he continued to remain under water, the man panicked. What had he done? He had endangered the life of this youngster. He wanted to go into the mikvah, clothes and all, to bring up the child, but he felt paralyzed, as if bound by some unforeseen force. As time passed, he forgot his anguish about the *poritz* and thought only, "Please, G-d, let the child come out alive!"

After what appeared to the man as an eternity, Zeide R' Motele emerged from the mikvah. "You may go home," he said to the man. "The *poritz* will not harm you."

Several weeks later, the man returned and told the Cherkassy Zeide about the incident. "When I returned home, the *poritz's* hirelings were restoring the windows. The *poritz* said to me, 'All night I could not sleep. I felt as though someone was choking me. I thought that perhaps this was because I had been so cruel to you and your family. It was only after I sent my men to restore the windows that the choking stopped. You can have all the time you need to pay the rent.' "

The Cherkassy Zeide said, "He is jeopardizing himself prematurely. The intensity of prayer to bring about such salvation requires a degree of *mesiras nefesh* (self-sacrifice) that can endanger one's life."

Inasmuch as he was an orphan, Zeide R' Motele began putting on *tefillin* at age twelve, as is the custom. At age thirteen he was engaged to Raitza, the daughter of the *tzaddik* of Sanz, R' Chaim Halberstam. The *shidduch* was completed by an emissary of the *tzaddik*. When someone asked the *tzaddik* how he could take a husband for his daughter without personally meeting him, he responded, "My father-in-law (R' Baruch Frankel, author of the halachic works *Baruch Taam*) took me without meeting me. Furthermore, I know that my son-in-law shines like the bright sun, and learns Torah *lishma* (with total dedication)."

Before the wedding, the *tzaddik* of Sanz said to the Cherkassy Zeide, "My dear *mechuten*, I took the thousand rubles that I had promised as a dowry along with me. However, along the way I encountered many poor people and I gave all the money away for *tzeddakah* (which was typical for the *tzaddik*). If you want the money before the *chuppah* (marriage ceremony), we will have to delay it until I can raise a thousand rubles."

The Cherkassy Zeide asked for some time to think about it. The *tzaddik* of Sanz retired to his quarters and studied Torah. Soon there was a knock on the door. A messenger from the Cherkassy Zeide requested that the *tzaddik* come to the *chuppah.*

When the *tzaddik* of Sanz arrived, the Chekassy Zeide said, "My holy *mechuten*! After you left, I was alone with the *choson* (groom). My father appeared to me from *Gan Eden* and told me that I was not to cause my *mechuten* any aggravation. If the *mechuten* was able to bring my father to my grandson's wedding, I forgive the entire dowry."

It is customary among some chassidim that a married woman cut her hair very short. The Russian government, among its other anti-Jewish decrees, issued an edict forbidding this. When the Babba Raitza, who was moving from Sanz in Galicia to Hornosteipol in Russia, cut her hair, her father asked her why she was risking punishment by violating the edict. Babba Raitza said, "I am confident that Father will get this edict annulled." The *tzaddik* of Sanz replied, "If you have that kind of trust, then I, too, am confident that the edict will be annulled." Shortly thereafter, the edict was indeed revoked.

The *tzaddik* of Sanz requested that Zeide R' Motele stay with him, but the Cherkassy Zeide said that he could not be without him. The *tzaddik* asked his young son-in-law to visit him as often as possible. It is noteworthy that the *tzaddik* addressed his fifteen-year-old son-in-law with the respectful form of "you" (*ihr*) rather than with the familiar "you" (*du*). The young couple returned to Hornosteipol, where the Cherkassy Zeide was residing at the time. When he visited Sanz, the *tzaddik* would send some of his *chassidim* to his young son-in-law with their petitions. "His prayers are most effective," he said.

When the Cherkassy Zeide left Hornosteipol for Cherkassy, Zeide R' Motele accompanied him, and remained his disciple, together with R' Naftali Halberstam, a grandson of both the *tzaddik* of Sanz and the Cherkassy Zeide. The two were inseparable, spending the entire day in Torah study together. Zeide R' Motele held R' Naftali in very high esteem.

One time the two disagreed on the interpretation of a difficult portion of Talmud. R' Naftali argued convincingly for his interpretation, but Zeide R' Motele rebutted all his proofs until R' Naftali admitted that Zeide R' Motle's interpretation was correct. He went beyond admitting, even citing further proofs to Zeide R' Motele's position.

They continued their study well into the night, then both retired. But Zeide R' Motele could not sleep. He was tormented by the thought, "How could R' Naftali possibly have been wrong? His devotion to truth was so intense that he could not have harbored an incorrect interpretation." He then reviewed the subject very meticulously and concluded that R' Naftali's interpretation had indeed been right. Full of joy, he went to R' Naftali in the middle of the night to inform him that his interpretation was the correct one.

The two *chaverim* (friends) continued their study of Torah uninterruptedly, even when R' Naftali fell ill. One time, Zeide R' Motele said, "Tomorrow we will start a new topic in Talmud." R' Naftali responded, "Tomorrow I will be in *Gan Eden*." He died the next day, at the age of twenty-six. Zeide R' Motele was inconsolable over the loss of his Torah partner.

Inasmuch as R' Naftali had died childless, his widow had to be released with the *chalitzah* ritual (*Deuteronomy* 25:7-10) so that she would be free to remarry. R' Naftali's father, R' Yechezkel Halberstam of Shinuvi, and his son, R' Moshe, came to Cherkassy and the ritual was carried out by the *beis din* (rabbinical court). The Torah scholars engaged in Torah discussions during the procedure. Throughout the ritual, Zeide R' Motele sat silent, staring into space.

R' Yechezkel was surprised that Zeide R' Motele did not partictate in the Torah discussion, to which he replied, "What Torah dicussion?" Zeide R' Motele said he had not heard a thing. "R' Naftali came down from *Gan Eden* to witness the *chalitzah*," he said. "His face radiated brightly, and I could not take my eyes off him. I did not hear any Torah discussion."

One time, the Cherkassy Zeide became very ill, and physicians did not know what to do for him. He fell into a coma for several days, and Zeide R' Motele could not be persuaded to leave the bedside. One morning, just as suddenly as he had fallen ill, he came out of coma and said to Zeide R' Motele, "I know the source of my illness.

"The 365 Torah prohibitions and the 248 positive mitzvos correspond to the 365 tendons and the 248 organs in the body. The organs and the tendons receive their spiritual nutrients when one observes the mitzvos of the Torah. If one is derelict in any mitzvah, the corresponding physical part lacks its nutrition and is affected.

"During the days that I appeared to be unconscious, I was doing exacting soul-searching, and I discovered the cause of my illness. Because of my studies of the esoteric aspects of Torah, I had been derelict in adequate study of the Talmud. I, therefore, took a vow to learn eighteen chapters of the Mishnah between *Minchah* and *Maariv* every day. I have now corrected my dereliction, and I am now well." And with that, he arose from his bed and was in good health.

Soon thereafter, the Cherkassy Zeide said to Zeide R' Motele, "The time has come for you to be a Rebbe. Your place is in Hornosteipol, and you must go there."

Zeide R' Motele broke out in tears. "I am too young to assume such a responsibility," he said, "and I cannot leave the zeide."

"You must know," the Cherkassy Zeide said, "that positions of leadership are predetermined and do not overlap even for a moment. If you wish me to continue to live, you must leave here."

Zeide R'Motele had no choice but to move to Hornosteipol. He came to Hornosteipol for *Shabbos Nachmu* (the week after *Tisha B'Av*), 1863. For six weeks, he did not give any Torah discourses. On the Shabbos of *Ki Savo*, he gave his first Torah discourse, and forty years later, on the Shabbos of *Ki Savo*, he gave his last Torah discourse. Later that night he died.

The older *chassidim* who remembered Zeide R' Motele's first Torah discourse said that the first and last were like the opening and closing chapters of a book.

Chapter 11
As Rebbe in Hornosteipol

The stories I heard from Zeide R' Leibele and from the *chassidim* of Zeide R' Motele are particularly dear to me. They are first-hand, eyewitness accounts that have not undergone the changes that often occur when the account of an incident goes through many hands. Here is one of them.

Zeide R' Motele had a *chassid*, Nechemiah of Ignatovke. Nechemiah had once been wealthy, but lost his fortune and was deeply in debt. His creditors pressed him to repay the money, but he had no way of doing so.

One day one of his creditors said to him, "Nechemiah, I have a way in which you can pay me and your other creditors, and you may have something left over for yourself. The other day I was traveling through the woods and I came across a body of a man who had been killed by a falling tree. I took his *pass* (official identification document), and I have it here.

"You are very clever at copying a signature. You can write a note to the bank authorizing them to lend three thousand rubles (a huge sum) to the bearer, and forge the signature of the *poritz*. When they ask for your identification, you will hand them the *pass* of the dead man. When the note comes due, they will go after him for the payment."

"Are you crazy?" Nechemiah said. "You want me to commit forgery? That is punishable by permanent exile to Siberia!"

"Don't be a fool," the man said. "There is no way you could be detected. Think of it. You may pay off your debts and start off in business anew. This is the opportunity you've been waiting for!"

The thought of being free of his creditors was irresistible. Nechemiah put the dead man's *pass* in his pocket. He wrote out the instructions to give the bearer the requested loan, and signed the name of the *poritz*. The two headed for the bank.

When the bank official asked Nechemiah for identification, he put his hand into his pocket, but by mistake pulled out *his own pass*. It was too late. He could not put it back and take out the other *pass* without giving himself away. The official approved the loan and gave Nechemiah the three thousand rubles.

R' Mordechai Dov of Hornosteipol (Zeide R' Motele)

Nechemiah's creditor was waiting for him outside the bank. "I'm in deep trouble," Nechemiah said. "I must return the money immediately. The note is in my name." He related what had happened. "If I don't get that note back, I'm doomed to a life sentence in Siberia."

"Don't give me that story," the creditor said. "You just want to keep the money for yourself and not pay your debts. Now give me the money that you owe me." Nechemiah had no choice but to give it to the man.

Nechemiah planned to somehow raise the money and pay off the note before the due date. However, when there were needs at home and when he was hounded by creditors, he spent a little here, a little there, until he was left with seven hundred rubles. Not knowing how he could ever raise such a huge sum, he went to Hornosteipol, to Zeide R' Motele, for advice.

Zeide R' Motele was an extremely gentle person. No one had ever heard him raise his voice. This time, however, he rebuked Nechemiah in a very loud voice. How dare he be dishonest and obtain the money by deceit! This was a gross violation of the Ten Commandments!

Nechemiah absorbed the reprimand, then broke down in tears. "I know I was wrong," he said. "But now what is to happen to me? Am I to spend the rest of my life in Siberia? What about my wife and children? Why should they suffer?"

"I'll see what I can do," Zeide R' Motele said. He took the remaining money from Nechemiah and sent him home. He then called in his son, Zeide R' Leibele. "Go to Kiev, and contact our friends who are wealthy. I need them to lend me 2300 rubles."

Zeide R' Leibele returned from Kiev empty handed. For whatever reasons, he had not been able to raise the money. Zeide R' Motele said to him, "You might as well return the remaining seven hundred rubles to Nechemiah. It makes no difference anymore."

Days went by, and the due date was approaching. Nechemiah came to Hornosteipol, and Zeide R' Motele told him to remain. Nechemiah had arranged for transportation to flee across the border, but Zeide R' Motele told him to wait.

On the eve before the due date, Nechemiah pleaded with Zeide R' Motele to give him permission to flee, but Zeide R' Motele refused. All that night Nechemiah remained in the Beis Midrash saying *Tehillim*. Zeide R' Motele was secluded in his study, and could be heard pacing to and fro all night.

After dawn, Zeide R' Motele emerged and said to Nechemiah, "Go to the bank and ask for the note. Tell them you want to pay it off."

Nechemiah was perplexed. He expected Zeide R' Motele to give him the money. When none was forthcoming, he said, "But, Rebbe…"

"Go to the bank and tell them you want to pay off the note," Zeide R' Motele said. Again Nechemiah started to question where the money was. Zeide R' Motele repeated his words a third time.

The gabbai (Zeide's aide), overhearing the dialogue, moved in and took Nechemiah by the hand. "If the Rebbe tells you to do something, go do it!" he said with vehemence.

Nechemiah was beside himself. He felt he was going to his doom. However, he had no choice. Trembling, he went to the bank and asked for the note. After some delay, the teller returned. "Just how do you spell your name?" he asked.

Nechemiah began to feel a bit relieved. He spelled his name clearly. The teller returned, saying, "I'm sorry. We cannot find any note with that name. Are you sure that it was under this name?"

Nechemiah developed a bold attitude. "Look here," he said. "I am a busy businessman and I do not have any time to waste. I cannot dilly-dally around here. I have to leave the country, and I will be away for at least a year, perhaps even two years. I do not wish to be held responsible for the bank's ineptness in filing documents. I may return after two years to find that I am being held liable for a loan that I wished to pay off. Who knows? Two years from now I may not be in a position to pay it off. I want you to make out a document stating that I was here to pay off this loan, that you could not find it, and that therefore you will not press for collection if you do find it when I return." The teller complied, and gave Nechemiah a copy of the document.

Nechemiah walked out a free man.

This is not a story I read someplace. Zeide R' Leibele was a participant in it and told it to me in authentic detail.

Another story is one I heard from two independent eyewitnesses: Zeide R' Leibele and a *chassid*, Zelig Chepovetzky.

Zelig was a resident of Ivankov, a village not far from Hornosteipol. Zelig's father, Moshe, once complained to Zeide R' Motele that he had no means of a livelihood. Zeide R' Motel said, "Moshke, become a doctor."

Becoming a doctor was as unrealistic as flying to the moon (in those days). Jews were not easily admitted to medical school, and furthermore, Moshke was virtually illiterate in Russian. Nevertheless, the Rebbe's word was not to be ignored. Moshke hired himself out to the local physician to carry his medicine bag. He would note the patient's symptoms and what the doctor prescribed. After a while, he began treating people himself. Lo and behold! All of Moshke's patients recovered. People said that the angel of healing, Raphael, accompanied Moshke. My father told me that the professors of medicine in the Kiev university had great respect for Moshke, calling him "our esteemed colleague!" *Chassidim*, of course, dubbed him "Moshke Professor."

Many of the chassidic communities in the Ukraine subjected themselves to the authority of a Rebbe. They did not engage a rabbi or *shochet* or adopt any important policy without the Rebbe's approval. The village of Ivankov was under Zeide R' Motele's authority.

The economy of Ivankov was heavily dependent on its yeast factories. When Passover came, the proprietors sold the factories to a non-Jew and continued their operation during Passover. On a number of occasions, Zeide R' Motele told the owners that they must shut down the factories during Passover. However, the owners were defiant.

Inasmuch as the *chassidim* remained at home to conduct the family *seder*, it was customary that they visited the Rebbe on *Shabbos Hagodol*, the Shabbos preceding Passover.

Shabbos morning, at the *kiddush*, Zeide R' Motele was not in his usual cheerful demeanor. He sharply chastised the people of Ivankov for defying his instructions. "I have repeatedly told you to close the factories on Passover. I must warn you that the halachah requires that *chometz* on Passover must be disposed of by fire."

Moshke spoke up. "But Rebbe," he said, "I'm not involved in this. I have nothing to do with yeast. Why are you upset with me?"

Zeide R' Motele said, "No, Moshke, I did not mean you."

Zeide R' Leibele told me that on the first night of Passover, Zeide R' Motele would normally hurry to the *seder* in order to eat the *afikomon* before midnight. This time, he was clearly upset, and was pacing back and forth, finally beginning the *seder* quite late. In the midst of the *seder*, a group of people from Ivankov, including Moshke's son, Zelig, entered. Zeide R' Motele did not wait to hear them out. He went into his study, and on Yom Tov took some money and gave it to them to buy the essentials for the village. He sent several people to the citizens of Hornosteipol with instructions to donate whatever food they can, along with blankets and clothes, and load wagons to carry everything to Ivankov.

Zelig told me that toward evening a fire had broken out in Ivankov and spread rapidly. The townsfolk tried to save some of their belongings by carrying them across the river that ran through the town, but the fire jumped the river and razed the entire town. Only one house was left unscathed: that of Moshke Professor, to whom Zeide R' Motele had said, "I did not mean you."

Zelig was an octogenarian when I was an adolescent. I repeatedly asked him to tell me this remarkable story with all its details, and he never refused. Zeide R' Leibele told it to me, too, but Zelig's account was more interesting. He would cry profusely as he related watching the town go up in flame, sparing only his father's house. He would end his narration with, "The Rebbe burned down our town, but he then built it up again."

One of Zeide R' Motele's *chassidim* who made *aliyah* to Israel many years ago related the following story.

A Jewish grain merchant had as a competitor an ardent anti-Semite. One time the two were together at an inn. The competitor had an attendant with him, and when no one noticed, he put poison into the attendant's drink. The attendant began screaming with pain and dropped dead. The anti-Semite said that he saw the Jew poison the drink. "He was going to kill me as well to eliminate me as a competitor," he said. The police were summoned, and the Jew, knowing how the scales of Czarist Russian justice were tipped against Jews, ran for his life.

In desperation, the Jew came to Zeide R' Motele. After waiting in line for his turn to see the rebbe, he poured out his sad tale to Zeide R' Motele, who told him, "Go buy a first-class ticket on the *parichad* (the steamboat that traveled up and down the Dnieper River)."

The Jew was beside himself. How could he return home? He was certain to be arrested and accused of murder! Nevertheless, his trust in the Rebbe was great. He bought a first-class ticket on the ship.

Full of anxiety and dread, the Jew sat down in the empty first-class cabin and began pouring out his broken heart over *Tehillim* (*Psalms*), crying uncontrollably. So engrossed was he in his prayers that he did not notice the entry of two distinguished looking individuals, one of whom was a pathologist who was on his way to do an inquest on the death of the attendant. Curious as to why this Jew was weeping, they asked him what his trouble was. The Jew told them of what had happened, and that he was going to be punished for a crime committed by the other merchant.

The two were impressed by the sincerity of the Jew's account. Arriving in town, they visited the merchant and invited him to a tavern. When the latter was inebriated, the pathologist began telling him about all the troubles he had suffered from Jews. The merchant was only too happy to tell him how he had rid himself of a pesky Jewish competitor.

Entering the courtroom for the inquest, the Jew realized that the two people in the first class cabin were the pathologist and the judge! The pathologist reported the merchant's confession, and the Jew was proven innocent.

For the sake of completion, I will include a story that I wrote in *Not Just Stories*. This story is especially dear to me, because my father was personally involved in it, and I thus have a first-hand account.

My father told me that for an observant Jew to be conscripted into the czarist army was nothing less than disastrous. The czarist army was not the United States army, where one's religious practices are given consideration. Furthermore, anti-Semitism was rampant even among the civilian population, and to be a Jew in the military was virtually to risk one's life. There was just as great a danger, or perhaps even greater, of being killed by one's "buddies" than by the enemy. There was no deferment for Divinity students, and the only way to avoid conscription was through personal contact with an official, which often meant securing one's freedom with a bribe.

When my father became of draft age, Zeide R' Leibele, who had succeeded Zeide R' Motele as rebbe of Hornosteipel, tried to contact influential people who might arrange a deferment for him, but all efforts proved futile. He then thought of trying to explain to the medical officer who was authorized to reject recruits on the basis of health considerations that my father's rigorous religious observance and his refusal to eat non-kosher food would soon result in physical deterioration, which would render him unfit for military service. Zeide R' Leibele was told that this medical officer, Dr. Primakow, was an assimilated Jew who had little sympathy for religion, and there was no reason to expect that he would be willing to help. Nevertheless, since there was nothing else to do, Zeide R' Leibele felt that it was worth a try. Accompanied by his gabbai and my father, he went to Kiev to see Dr. Primakow.

When the secretary told the doctor who the people were that wished to see him, he came to the waiting room, looked at Zeide R' Leibele and said, "This is not the Rebbe of Hornosteipel. He is a much shorter person." The gabbai explained that the doctor must be referring to to the previous rebbe of Hornosteipel who had died, and that Zeide R' Leibele was his son who had succeeded him. Dr. Primakow escorted the three into his office, and Zeide R' Leibele posed his request.

To his great astonishment, Dr. Primakow listened attentively and appeared to be genuinely interested. When Zeide

R' Leibele finished his explanation, Dr. Primakow said, "I understand. Normally, I would not give a second thought to such considerations, but I do feel that I am indebted to your father, and I should return a favor." Zeide R' Leibele was bewildered. He was unable to imagine what kind of indebtedness Dr. Primakow could possibly have had to Zeide R' Motele.

"When I was a young doctor," Dr. Primakow continued, "I was assigned to physically examine the draftees. I travelled from town to town to the various draft boards. On one such trip, I lodged at an inn in Hornosteipel, and all I heard people talking about was the greatness and the saintliness of their rebbe.

"I had no interest whatever in religion and no use for a rebbe, but the exalted praise he received aroused my curiosity, and I simply wanted to see who this person was. I was ushered into the rebbe's study, and he greeted me very warmly. I had the strange feeling that he was looking right through me, yet his eyes were so soft and comforting that I did not feel uneasy. It was indeed a pleasant experience.

"As I rose to leave, the rebbe said to me, 'I hope that you will never cause harm to any Jew, and I give you my blessing that a non-Jew should never cause you any harm.' I thanked the rebbe for his kind words, and as I left, he escorted me down a long corridor, all the way to the door. As I was about to step out, he said, 'Remember, you must not do any harm to a Jew, and a non-Jew will never harm you.' The repetition of the remark irritated me. What need was there to say it twice and to urge me to remember it?

"As you well know, we were often approached by draftees who wished to buy their freedom from military service. All of us were on the take, but we were concerned that if we were caught accepting a bribe, that could result in severe punishment. I, therefore, had concluded that I would keep the number of bribes to a minimum, accepting only a few very substantial bribes.

"In one town, I was approached by a young Jewish boy who explained how difficult it would be for him to serve in the military because of his religious observance. '300 rubles,' I said.

The young boy was taken aback. '300 rubles?' he said. 'My family could never raise anywhere near that amount. Perhaps we could manage 25 rubles.' I stood firm. '300 rubles,' I said. 'When you have that amount you may return. Otherwise, don't bother me.'

"A while later, another young man, a non-Jew, asked to be deferred. I told him my price was 300 rubles, and he said that was satisfactory. His father had a number of local merchants with whom he did business, and he would return in a few hours with the money.

"Just opposite my office was that of another military medical examiner, an ardent anti-Semite, and although I was not a practicing Jew, he hated me nonetheless. When the second young man returned with the money, the Jewish boy was still standing in the corridor, somehow hoping that I would reconsider. He saw the non-Jew mistakenly knock on the door of the other doctor's office, and when he entered and saw that he was in the wrong office, he excused himself and stepped back, whereupon the doctor said, 'Don't go away. Just come here.

" 'You were probably looking for Dr. Primakow, weren't you?' he said. 'I can take care of that for you. We are all in this together. How much did he ask you for?' The young man told him that he had brought 300 rubles. 'Let me see the money,' the doctor said.

"The Jewish boy observed all this through the open door, and saw that the doctor counted the money, then made some markings on the money and returned it to the young man saying, 'Yes, it is the right amount. You can go across the hall and give it to Dr. Primakow.' This was clearly done in order to trap me as having accepted a bribe.

"After the young man brought me the money and left, the Jewish boy knocked on my door. 'Do you have the necessary amount?' I asked. 'No,' he said, 'but I did not come this time on my behalf. I came on your behalf,' and he proceeded to tell me what he had observed.

""I took out the money and noted that there were indeed identifiable markings on it. I then said to the Jewish boy, 'Don't worry. You will be deferred.'

"Several days later, when the young men appeared for their medical examinations, I noted that the other doctor was in high spirits. I knew that he was gleefully anticipating the opportunity to expose me for having accepted a bribe. When I examined the Jewish boy, I put the stethescope on his chest and exclaimed, 'You are no specimen for our army. I'm surprised you're even alive,' and I dismissed him.

"Soon afterward, the non-Jew came for his exam. I noticed the sneer on the other doctor's face as I began my examination. I listened carefully to the young man's heart and lungs and said, 'Very healthy. You will make a fine soldier.'

"The other doctor was taken aback. 'Are you sure he is healthy?' he asked. 'Perhaps you should listen to his heart again. He looks somewhat asthenic (weak) to me.'

"I said, 'No. I think he is fine. If you think otherwise, you may examine him.

" 'Let me tell you something,' I said. 'This young man had the audacity to try to bribe me to defer him, and he offered me 300 rubles.' I then took the 300 rubles out of my pocket and threw them on the desk in front of the members of the draft board. 'There you have the bribe. Let no one say that the czar's officers are corrupt.'

"I then understood what the rebbe had meant. I was to avoid harming any Jew, and I would be blessed that no non-Jew would harm me. His words and blessings had come true, and I had narrowly escaped being trapped and convicted of bribery. I owe the rebbe a favor in return for his blessing." Then, turning to my father, the doctor said, "This young man is hardly the kind that would serve well in the army," and with that he dismissed him.

(When my father told me this story, I asked, "Didn't the fulfillment of Zeide's *berachah* have any impact on the doctor to make him more religious?" My father explained that the Midrash states that when the Israelites saw the Reed Sea split before their eyes and when they crossed the divided waters on dry land, they nevertheless carried an idol along with them. "That is the cunning and the power of the *yet-*

zer hara. A person can be confronted with incontrovertible evidence of G-d's presence and might nevertheless deny Him.")

My uncle, R' Shlomo Halberstam, the late Bobover Rebbe, related the following story.

> Prior to a trip to Mexico, the newspaper had written about his forthcoming visit, and among other things, mentioned that he was a descendant of the Rebbe of Hornosteipol.
>
> A gentleman came up to see him, a man who was totally alienated from Yiddishkeit, and had not been in a shul for years, even on Yom Kippur. He was interested in meeting the rebbe because as a child, his father, who was a *chassid* of the rebbe, had taken him to Hornosteipol.
>
> "Do you recall anything your father told you about the Rebbe of Hornosteipol?" my uncle asked.
>
> "Only this one thing. One time my father came to see the rebbe and found him to be dancing. The rebbe said, 'You are no doubt puzzled why I am dancing. Today is the coronation of Czar Nicholas II (this was about 1894). This is the last czar Russia will ever have. It is customary that when parents marry off their *muzhinke* (youngest and last child), they have a special dance. This czar is our *muzhinke*. That is why I am dancing.' "
>
> It wasn't until 1917 that the communist revolution put an end to the czarist dynasty.

> My father's brother, Uncle Nochum, told me that Zeide R' Motele's followers from Ignatovke once complained to him about their bitter lot. The *poritz* of their fiefdom appointed a Jew who had converted to Christianity as the local governor, and who relentlessly persecuted the local Jews even more than the non-Jewish anti-Semites.
>
> One day Zeide R' Motele came to Ignatovke and was greeted by a throng of *chassidim*. As the procession made its way through the town, Zeide R' Motele instructed the driver to stop in front of a house, which was the residence of the governor.

Hearing the commotion outside, the governor went out to see what was happening. To the astonishment of the *chassidim*, Zeide R' Motele went into the house of the governor. The *chassidim* were even further surprised that the governor followed him, and a few of them made their way inside.

Zeide R' Motele seated himself at a table opposite the governor. The *chassidim* were certain that he was going to plead in their behalf, but he did not utter a single word. Zeide R' Motele just stared at the governor for a while, then rose and left the house. The bewildered *chassidim* did not know what to make of this.

At Shalosh Seudos (the third Shabbos meal), on Shabbos although the room was dark, someone noticed that the governor had come in. After *Havdalah* (ritual at the closing of Shabbos), Zeide R' Motele had a private session with the governor for three hours. The following day the governor, who had announced that his name was Avraham, threw away all his kitchen utensils and made his kitchen kosher.

In short, Avraham becam a complete *baal-teshuvah* and did his utmost to compensate for the suffering he had inflicted upon the community. But within the year, Avraham the *baal-teshuvah* died, and the community mourned the loss of one who had become their benefactor.

One day, Zeide R' Motele was sitting with his *chassidim* and said, "Nu, what do you say about Avraham? He was a true *baal-teshuvah*, wasn't he?" All the *chassidim* concurred.

There was one *chassid*, however, who had suffered severely from the governor's persecution, who said, "What! That *rasha* (wicked person) who had caused us so much grief?"

Zeide R' Motele turned pale. He sank into deep meditation and then said, "Unanimous opinions are suspect. It is good that there was one dissent. Now Avraham's soul can rest in peace."

Another incident in this vein occurred with an estranged Jew who lived in one of the *shtetls* in the province which

abided by Zeide R' Motele's leadership. At every opportunity, this person would make life miserable for the
observant community. When they needed to cut branches
for the covering of the *succah* he would tell the local authorities that the *chassidim* were defacing the city by
deforestation. When they built their *succahs*, he would report them as fire hazards. The *chassidim* often complained
to Zeide R' Motele about the suffering this man was
causing them.

One day, in the anteroom of Zeide R' Motele's study, there
was great commotion. This much-despised Jew was asking
for an audience with the rebbe. After much deliberation, the
chassidim permitted him to enter.

The man told Zeide R' Motele that he had just returned
from a business trip. He had found one community in turmoil over the following incident. The body of a man had
washed ashore, and inasmuch as he could not be identified,
he was buried in a pauper's grave in a non-Jewish cemetery.
Weeks later, it was discovered that a Jew had been on a boat
trip and was never heard from again. It was evident that the
unidentified man was Jewish, and the Jewish community insisted on the body being disinterred and buried in a Jewish
cemetery. This resulted in a violent reaction from the non-
Jewish community.

"I have my private reasons for not observing Judaism," the
man said. "However, even though I am not living a Jewish
life, I wish to be buried among Jews. How can I be sure that
if my body were to surface somewhere, that I would be
buried in a Jewish cemetery?"

Zeide R' Motele instructed the man to wear a *talis katan* (a
small four-cornered garment with *tzitzis* [fringes]) at all times.
The man promptly bought several pairs. Several weeks later,
this Jew began making sporadic appearances at Zeide R'
Motele's Beis Midrash, apparently observing with great intensity what was happening. Eventually he asked Zeide R'
Motele what he can do for *teshuvah*, to compensate for his deviation from Judaism and the grief he had imposed on the
Jewish community.

Zeide R' Motele pointed out to his *chassidim* the enormous significance of a single mitzvah, even when the motive is not of the highest quality. The mitzvah of wearing *tzitzis* had brought this errant Jew back to his source.

Zeide R' Leibele told me about a rather remarkable episode.

> One day, Zeide R' Motele suddenly lost his vision. He would have R' Chaim of Oster (my father's Talmud teacher) read Torah to him. My father told me that R' Chaim was erudite in Kabbalah as well as in halachah. Zeide R' Leibele was, therefore, surprised to overhear that when R' Chaim was reading Zohar, Zeide R' Motele said, "Chaim, just say the letters. I'll put the words together myself." Apparently, R' Chaim's knowledge of Zohar did not reach Zeide R' Motele's standard.
>
> Then one day Zeide R' Motele said to Zeide R' Leibele, "I don't think I can take this much more. It has been enough." Later that day Zeide R' Motele was observed reading from a *sefer* by himself. One time, Zeide R' Leibele took a particular volume on Kabbalah from the bookshelf. Zeide R' Motele said, "Put it back. I'm afraid that it was the cause of my loss of vision."

After Zeide R' Motele returned from a trip, Zeide R' Leibele unpacked the *seforim* he had bought. He smiled as he saw among them the *siddur* of the Vilna Gaon. "What are you smiling about?" Zeide R' Motele asked. Zeide R' Leibele responded, "In past years this *siddur* could not be found in the home of a *chassid*, and today it is in the home of a rebbe."

Zeide R' Motele said, "Everyone is amazed at the Gaon's enormous knowledge of Talmud. That does not begin to compare to his knowledge of Kabbalah." Indeed, the Gaon's disciple, R' Chaim of Volozhin, attested to this very point.

> One time, the Cherkassy Zeide sent for Zeide R' Motele to come to Cherkassy. After spending Shabbos together, the Cherkassy Zeide took him to the room where the Babba, who was ill, was in bed. Zeide R' Motele's gabbai, R' Raphael,

managed to conceal himself in a closet and related overhearing the following dioalogue.

The Cherkassy Zeide said, "The Babba and I have a *din-Torah*. Normally, the *dayan* (magistrate) is seated and the litigants stand. Due to our age, however, you will permit us to sit. We want you as a *dayan* because we know that your judgment will be honored by G-d.

"The Babba and I disagree as to which of us should die first…"

Tears welled up in Zeide R' Motele's eyes. "I should make such a decision?" he interrupted. "I don't want to hear this. The Zeide and Babba will live to greet Mashiach."

The Cherkassy Zeide said, "I agree to that, but if our time comes before that, we should determine who dies first. You realize that it is not appropriate for me that a strange woman should come in to take care of the house and prepare meals."

The Babba spoke up, "Tell me what sin I have done that I should be punished with having to hear *kiddush* from a stranger."

Zeide R' Motele asked for time to think. He later said, "As far as a judgment is concerned, the Babba is right. But how can I go against the Zeide's wishes? So, after you have lived a long life, you should both go to the Eternal World within the same year."

And so it was. Six months after the Babba died, the Cherkassy Zeide died on the thirteenth day of Elul, 5636 (1876).

When Zeide R' Motele's daughter, Yocheved, was due to have a child, her husband, R' Elisha Halberstam of Gorlitz, asked his father-in-law for suggestions for a name. Zeide R' Motele said, "Mendl." R' Elisha asked, "And if it's a girl?" Zeide R' Motele answered, "Then you send me a telegram." Incidentally, I knew R' Mendl very well.

Zeide R' Leibele's first child was a girl, Devorah. When she was an infant, Zeide R' Motele asked him, "How is your *bas yechidah* (only daughter)?" Zeide R' Leibele said, "I knew right then that I would not have any more daughters." Indeed, he then had four sons.

After the Cherkassy Zeide's death, Zeide R' Motele felt that his great uncle, R' Dovid of Talna, was the *tzaddik hador* (leading *tzaddik* of the generation). He frequently visited Talna and would often say, "In Talna one can gather heaps of *yiras shamayim* (fear of Heaven)."

R' Dovid would often conceal lofty thoughts in ordinary conversation. Zeide R' Motele quoted the prayer, "And David blessed G-d before the eyes of the congregation. David said, 'Blessed are You…' " He then referred to his great uncle, saying, "David was always blessing G-d, but in the eyes of the congregation, it appeared that he was just saying things."

One Chanukah, Zeide R' Motele was in Talna. As R' Dovid entered to kindle the Chanukah lights, he stopped and said to one man, "You are much taller than your wife. When you talk to her, do you bend down toward her or does she try to reach up to you?" Without waiting for an answer, R' Dovid recited the *berachos* for the Chanukah lights.

The *chassidim* gathered aound Zeide R' Motele for an explanation. Zeide R' Motele said, "Perhaps my uncle was referring to the Talmudic statement, 'The *Shechinah* (Divine presence) never descended within ten handbreadths of the earth' (*Succah* 5a). The exception to this is Chanukah, because halachah requires that the lights be within ten handbreadths of the ground. Inasmuch as the Chanukah lights radiate the Divine presence, the *Shechinah* does descend there. The Ari z"l says that the secret of Chanukah is contained in the Talmudic statement, 'If your wife is short, bend down and whisper to her.' This is what my uncle meant about bending down to communicate. On Chanukah, the Divine presence descends to communicate with Israel."

The following day, R' Dovid again made a cryptic comment to one of his *chassidim* before lighting the Chanukah candles.

He then turned to Zeide R' Motele and said, "Today you will not be able to reveal the meaning of this as you did yesterday." Zeide R' Motele was amazed at the evident encyclopedic knowledge of R' Dovid.

R' Dovid always had a cheerful disposition, in spite of the many tragedies he suffered. All of his children died in their infancy. Only one child, R' Motele, survived into adulthood, and he, too, died in his father's lifetime. R' Motele, too, lost ten of his eleven children, and only one, R' Nochum, survived. Such losses of children and grandchildren would have totally crushed any other person. The greatness of R' Dovid can be gathered from his acceptance of the Divine judgment with a faith and trust that allowed him to retain his good cheer.

Even as a youngster, it was evident that R' Motele was exceptionally spiritual. He devoted all his energies to redeeming Jews from imprisonment by the *poritzim.* On one of these travels he was exposed to the bitter cold for many hours. He developed a lung inflammation which turned into a chronic lung disease, which led to his premature death.

When R' Dovid heard of his son's illness, he visited him and said, "If you accept upon yourself to assume a position as a rebbe and perpetuate our lineage, I will be able to secure additional years of life for you." R' Motele refused the offer. He wished his Divine service to remain private, and he would not sacrifice this to expose himself as a rebbe even at the cost of his life.

When R' Motele's health deteriorated, he was taken for treatment to Kiev. On the way, they stopped in a village, Bahpoli, where he died at age twenty-nine. When his mother learned of the death of her only surviving child, she wept inconsolably. R' Dovid then said to her:

"My father (R' Mordechai of Czernoble) once traveled near Bahpoli, and went into a deep meditative state. The roughness of the road caused such a jarring of the coach that his head struck the wall, lacerating his skull, but this did not arouse him from his meditation. As they entered the village, he repeated several times, 'Bah Poli,' which was similar to the Russian words meaning, field of G-d. 'G-d wants this to be my resting place, but I do not concur. It will be the resting place of someone who will carry my name.' " When R' Dovid's wife heard that her father-in-law had prophesied that her son would be buried in Bahpoli, she was somewhat comforted.

When R' Motele's condition worsened in Bahpoli, they sent a telegram to R' Dovid in Talna. R' Dovid had secluded himself in his study and had gone to sleep. R' Dovid was a light sleeper, and his wife insisted that he be woken to pray for their son. However, R' Dovid could not be aroused, even when several *chassidim* stood him upright. His wife shouted to him, "Why don't you intercede to save the life of our only child?" R' Dovid opened his eyes and said, "Am I instead of G-d? We must praise G-d for the bad just as we do for the good."

The following day, one of R' Dovid's *chassidim* was to make a *bris* for a grandson. He asked R' Dovid what he should name the child, and R' Dovid said, "Wait a bit." Soon after that, word arrived that R' Motele had died. R' Dovid said to the *chassid*, "There you have your answer. You have someone to name him after."

R' Dovid then said, "When the High Priest, Aaron, lost his two sons, the Torah says, '*Vayidom Aharon*,' Aaron was silent (*Leviticus* 10:3). *Vayidom* also means that Aaron turned himself into a *domem*, an inanimate object. Because feeling grief would deter him from the Divine service, he rendered himself inanimate." This was how R' Dovid reacted to the tragedy of losing his only, beloved son.

Zeide R' Motele wrote a letter of consolation to R' Dovid.

I can feel your pain at the loss of your beloved son. Our sinful generation did not merit him.

Your sufferings are pangs of love. The Talmud says that the Tanna who lost his children was consoled when his wife told him that G-d had entrusted them with precious items for safekeeping, and that they had returned the items to their

Owner intact. Your consolation is that you, too, returned his precious soul intact.

I am confident that the sprig he left over will be raised by your holiness, and you will see blessed generations from him. And to him I am sending as a gift a garment from my saintly grandfather (the Chekassy Zeide)."

The "sprig," R' Menachem Nochum, indeed becme a chassidic leader. Such was the mettle of the *tzaddikim* that inspired Zeide R' Motele.

Chapter 12
Torah, Avodah and Gemilas Chassadim

Torah, Avodah and Gemillas Chassadim are the three pillars which, the Talmud says, are the foundation of the world (*Ethics of the Fathers* 1:2). Zeide R' Motele said that every person is a world in microcosm, and everyone must embody these three features.

Zeide R' Motele's enormous Torah erudition can be seen from his halachic works. His devotion to G-d in prayer and performance of mitzvos was intense, yet not outwardly apparent.

> One time the great Talmudist and leader of Hungarian Jewry, R' Chaim Elazar of Munkacz, observed Zeide R' Motele praying *Minchah*. He stood perfectly still through a long *Amidah*, after which the Rabbi of Munkacz noted that his clothes were saturated with perspiration, as if he had been doing exhaustive physical labor.
>
> The Rabbi of Munkacz commented, "I always had difficulty understanding the Talmudic statement that the phrase *ulavdo bechol levavchem* (serve G-d with all your heart) refers to *tefillah*

(prayer), which is *avodah shebelev* (service of the heart). What kind of 'work' is prayer? After seeing the *tefillah* of the Hornosteipoler Rebbe, I understand that silent prayer can be every bit as exhausting as physical exertion."

ספר

עמק החכמה

ספר זה קראתיו עמק החכמה . נימ' שמי עם ב' תיבות

מעשהו לבאר דקדוקי מקראות להיות דיבור על אופניו נדרש כמין
חומר . ע"פ דברי חז"ל אשר הם כמסמרות נטיעות . תילי תילי הלכות .
וליתא מידי דלא רמיזי באורייתא . והתורה נדרשת באופנים שונים . לכל
אחד כפי אשר קבל חלקו בנעימים . וד' יאיר עיני בהורתו ולעשות רצונו
בלבב שלם אמן .

ברפוס המשובח של השותהפים

הרבני הנגיד מוהר"ר יעקב נ"י ב"ר שלמה זל"ל הערשעננהארן ,
והרבני הנגיד מוהר"ר משה נ"י שניידמעסיר ,

בלובלין

שנת   תרמ"ד   לפ"ק

Emek Hachochmah, sefer by Zeide R' Motele

Zeide R' Motele taught that all service of G-d must be with *simchah*. Dejection, he said, is as lethal to the *neshamah* as cessation of the heartbeat is to the heart. As long as the heart is beating, there is hope for recovery. As long as a person is in *simchah*, he can recover spiritually.

In 1882, Zeide R' Motele's extensive library, which contained many treasured manuscripts, including a commentary on the Talmud Tractate *Kesubos* by R' Levi Yitzchok of Berditchev and a complete treatise of his own on the intricate subject of *shemos gittin* (correct spelling of names in a *get*), was destroyed by fire. The Torah discourses of the Cherkassy Zeide were also lost. His first reaction was a deep sigh and for a few moments his demeanor was sorrowful, but his cheerful expression quickly returned and he said to his *chassidim*, "The Talmud says that one must express gratitude to G-d when bad things happen just as when good things happen (*Berachos* 54a). Suppose I had won the sweepstakes. Wouldn't you have requested of me that I serve a L'Chaim? If that is how we would have celebrated a happy occasion, we must do the same now."

Half-heartedly, the *chassidim* asked for a L'Chaim. One *chassid* was bold enough to ask, "But the Rebbe's initial reaction was one of sorrow. Would the Rebbe have been sorrowful had he won the sweepstakes?"

Zeide R' Motele said, "The halachah is that if one swallows the bitter herbs at the *seder* without chewing them, one has not fulfilled the mitzvah of *maror*. One must feel the bitterness. When G-d causes something painful to happen, it has a purpose. One is supposed to feel the pain. However, one must realize that everything G-d does is good. It is like a bitter medication, which is unpleasant but beneficial.

"My first reaction, therefore, was to feel the pain of the loss, but then to realize that in ways beyond our understanding, it is really good."

At a later time, Zeide R' Motele said that in his library there was a Torah scroll which had markings at the ends of paragraphs, and he was researching to see whether it is a kosher Torah scroll. He mused,

"Perhaps that scroll was written by an apostate. Halachah requires that it be burned."

Zeide R' Motele was always in good cheer. Elsewhere (*Generation to Generation*), I wrote how my father would come into a room and exclaim, "*Lebedig, kinderlach, lebedig!*" (Be lively, my children, be lively.) I am certain he inherited this trait from Zeide R' Motele.

> Zeide R' Leibele told me that one time he notice that Zeide R' Motele was not in his usual cheerful mood. "Why is Father despondent?" he asked.
>
> Zeide R' Motele replied, "I am worried about all the debts I have incurred" (Zeide R' Motele would borrow extensively to give to *tzeddakah*).
>
> Zeide R' Leibele knew better. "That is not the reason. Father has never been saddened by money problems. Furthermore, if that were the problem, Father would have told me to go to Kiev to raise money to pay off the debt. It is something else."
>
> Zeide R' Motele said, "So what do you want? Should I tell you what is transpiring in heaven?"
>
> Zeide R' Leibele did not say another word. In relating this episode, he would say to me, "I have always regretted that I did not speak up and say that I indeed did want to know what was transpiring in heaven."

Zeide R' Motele, following the Baal Shem Tov's teachings, discouraged his *chassidim* from taking on additional fast days over and above those required by halachah. While he preached against indulgence and luxuries, he cited the Talmud quoted earlier that on Judgment Day a person will be held culpable for not partaking of the goods of the world. "Excessive fasting may lead to despondency. It is better to eat with the intention that the energy one derives from eating should be directed to the study of Torah and performance of mitzvos. However, one must be careful not to fall into indulgent behavior. Pursuit of pleasure creates a barrier between man and G-d."

Zeide R' Motele would quote his father-in-law, the *tzaddik* of Sanz, who was a model of *bitachon* and who said, "I can understand why merchants must keep a sum of money handy. A business opportunity may occur at any time for which they must be prepared. But people who are not merchants, how can they sleep at night when they have money in savings accounts, knowing that there are people who have no money for food or firewood?"

Zeide R' Motele used to tell the following story about the Alter Rebbe, one of whose grandchildren married into a wealthy family and received a handsome dowry. The Alter Rebbe was shocked to learn that his grandson had bought a silk *gartel* (sash) for fifteen rubles. How can a person be so extravagant?

The Alter Rebbe asked his grandson, "What have you done with the money of your dowry?" The grandson replied that he had given it to a businessman to invest for him.

"What kind of assurance do you have that your money is safe? Investments can go down just as they can go up. You would be better off giving the money to *tzeddakah*, which is an investment that can never go bad. Even the fifteen rubles for a silk *gartel* would have been better given to *tzeddakah*."

The grandson did not heed the Alter Rebbe's words. Several months later, the businessman's affairs failed, and the entire dowry was lost.

> The Alter Rebbe admonished his grandson for not listening to him. "One time," he said, "on the way to the Maggid of Mezeritch, I lodged at an inn in a small village. I asked the innkeeper why he was living in a place where there was no minyan (quorum of ten people for communal prayer). He said, 'What can I do? I have my livelihood here.' I said, 'Do you think that G-d, Who provides sustenance for all the Jews in a large community, will not be able to provide for one more?'
>
> "When I awoke the following morning," the Alter Rebbe continued, "I found that the innkeeper had packed all his belongings. 'I am moving into the town,' he said."

"The innkeeper had no idea who I was, but the fact that I was on my way to the Maggid of Mezeritch was enough for him to trust my words. Yet, when I explicitly told you what to do with your dowry, you did not have enough trust in me to do as I said! Just look where your desire for luxury has brought you. Fifteen rubles for a silk *gartel*, and a desire to get rich!"

A few words about R' Dan, who as Zeide R' Motele's gabbai (personal attendant) was his most dedicated *chassid*.

In relating this, my uncle said that it was unusual for a gabbai to be a fiery *chassid* of the Rebbe.

> A *chassid* once asked R' Dovid of Talna to accept him as a *gabbai*. R' Dovid denied the request, saying, "There are two types of people who do not have faith in the rebbe: some because they do not know him, or his gabbaim who know him too intimately. Why should I take a *chassid* who does believe in me and make him into a gabbai who will not believe in me?"

Not so with R' Dan.

R' Dan came from a wealthy family and was active in the family business. Numerous times he wished to write off his share of the business so that he could stay in Hornosteipol near his rebbe. Zeide R' Motele repeatedly discouraged him from doing so. On one occasion he cited the verse (*Numbers* 25:11) where G-d praises Pinchas for his zeal, "who avenged Me *in their midst*, and I did not consume the Children of Israel in My vengeance." He stressed the words "in their midst," explaining that Pinchas had not isolated himself from other Jews. He was zealous for G-d even though he was "in their midst," associating with them in their mundane activities. One may be zealous only if one intends to defend the community of Israel from destruction. Zeide R' Motele urged R' Dan to remain active in the business community and thereby influence people to observe Torah.

In spite of Zeide R' Motele's protestations, R' Dan left the family business, surrendering his share.

My uncle said that R' Dan said that anyone who did not see Zeide R' Motele would not believe that such a human being existed. "One could only imagine that this must have been what the *Kohen Gadol* (High Priest) looked like on Yom Kippur when he entered the Holy of Holies.

"It is needless to say what the Rebbe's *avodah* was like on Rosh Hashanah, Yom Kippur and Hoshana Rabbah. One could wash the floor with his tears. And then the *simchah* (joy) on Succos. On Simchas Torah the Rebbe danced without interuption for eight consecutive hours.

"Before dawn on the day after Simchas Torah, when I was certain the Rebbe would be totally exhausted, he handed me a long responsa that he had written that night. It involved the case of a woman who bore a child twelve months after her husband had been away. The Rebbe drew upon his encyclopedic knowledge of Talmud and all the commentaries to prove that it is possible for the gestation period to last twelve months and that the child was legitimate. This responsa caused considerable turmoil in the Torah world, but ultimately all the halachic authorities gave their approval.

"I could not imagine how after his intense physical exertion and sleep deprivation a person could concentrate to compose such a responsa. This was not done with mere mortal powers," R' Dan concluded.

> One time Zeide R' Motele needed a large sum of money for an urgent *tzeddakah*. He visited a wealthy man who lived in an opulent home with fine art and luxurious furnishings. The host greeted his distinguished guest warmly, and escorted him to his sitting room. To his host's surprise, Zeide R' Motele asked to see some of his valuable paintings. He marvelled at the beauty of each painting and inquired as to its value. The host was more than happy to show off his art collection, but knowing how precious each moment was to the *tzaddik*, he was perplexed at his taking so much time to view the artwork.
>
> After finishing his admiration of the art, Zeide R' Motele made similar inquiries about the furnishings and silver items. Following this, he told his host about the desperate situation for which he was collecting *tzeddakah*. Without hesitation, the host gave the *tzaddik* the amount he needed to alleviate the anguish of those in need.
>
> The host could not contain his curiosity. As he escorted the *tzaddik* to the door, he expressed his surprise that he took so much time to appreciate his artwork and furnishings. Zeide R' Motele explained, "Often, when I ask someone to part with a rather large sum of money, I detect some resistance. People

may not realize how fortunate they are to have such wealth. I wanted to make sure that you were aware how blessed you are to own so many fine things. That made it easier for you to give a substantial sum of money for those who have no food or a roof over their heads."

Zeide R' Motele's *ahavas Yisrael* is exemplified in the following incident.

Zeide R' Motele once developed a hiccough that persisted for three days in spite of all the home remedies to suppress it. Inasmuch as he suffered from heart disease, there was concern that his heart might be affected by this. Accompanied by his gabbai, he consulted a neurologist in Kiev. The neurologist said that the only way to stop the hiccough was by delivering a shock to the spinal cord. This was accomplished by heating an iron poker to glowing and running it down the spinal column. Zeide R' Motele said, "Nu," and proceeded to strip to the waist.

The doctor ran the red-hot poker down the spine, and when Zeide R' Motele did not utter a sound nor flinch a muscle, the doctor was perplexed. He reheated the poker and did a second application, this time with more pressure. When there was again no reaction, the doctor threw down the poker and exclaimed, "I can't believe this. He is some kind of angel rather than a human being. Why, a short while back I had a burly cossack here for this treatment, and I no sooner removed the poker from the fire than he jumped out the window. Here I have scalded him twice and he does not even react at all!"

Zeide R' Motele did not understand Russian and asked the gabbai to translate the doctor's comment. The gabbai said, "He said that the Rebbe is an angel," and went on to tell about the cossack who jumped out the window before he was even touched.

Zeide R' Motele said, "Sometimes a person comes to me with his *tzoros* (miseries) and I desperately want to help him, but there is nothing I can do. If I don't jump out the window from my anguish at that point, I certainly don't have to do so now."

Zeide R' Motele's *chesed* was without peer. I knew several of his *chassidim*, each of whom said, "The Rebbe never loved anyone else as much as he loved me," and this is how each one of his *chassidim* felt.

And just as much as he loved his *chassidim*, his *chassidim* loved him. This is demonstrated by the following story.

> When Zeide R' Motele died, there was competition about who gets the privilege to be buried next to him. R' Dan, who was Zeide R' Motele's personal attendant for years, claimed that he had earned this privilege. "Yankel the Rav," the local rabbi, claimed that his position gave him priority. They brought their dispute to Zeide R' Leibele, who ruled that the decision be left to G-d: Whoever died first would have the coveted grave.
>
> Zeide R' Leibele told me that if R' Dan ever took sick, Yankel the Rav would arrange for people to say *Tehillim (Psalms)* to pray for his recovery. He saw to it that no expense was spared to obtain the finest medical care. And if Yankel the Rav fell ill, R' Dan would do the same. Each was afraid that the other might die first.
>
> R' Dan died first. At this time, Zeide R' Leibele had moved from Hornosteipol to Kiev. One winter day, he insisted on going to Hornosteipol to Zeide R' Motele's gravesite. This was a time of unrest, and the family tried to discourage his making the trip. But Zeide R' Leibele was adamant. He arrived in Hornosteipol before Shabbos and learned that R' Dan was near death. R' Dan still was able to greet him, *Shalom aleichem.*
>
> R' Dan died on Shabbos, and Zeide R' Leibele attended his funeral. Zeide R' Leibele saw to it that R' Dan was buried next to his beloved rebbe. Had Zeide R' Leibele not been there, Yankel the Rov might have had R' Dan buried elsewhere.

How different things are today! Even Torah observant people may desire a beautiful dwelling, a summer home or a luxury car. R' Dan's and Yankel the Rav's greatest wish was to die first!

A *chassid* who had lost all his wealth once came to Zeide R' Motele, and after reading his *kvittel* (petition), Zeide R' Motele sighed deeply, then gave the man a large sum of money. He then read the *kvittel* a second time, and gave him a second large sum.

The *chassid* said, "Rebbe, I did not come to you for money."

Zeide R' Motele said, "The Torah says, 'Give, you shall give to him (the needy person), and your heart should not ache when you give to him' (*Deuteronomy* 15:10). What can I do? My heart still aches for you. I have to give you more money until my heart stops aching."

My aunt told me that after midnight, Zeide R' Motele used to give her money to take to a man who had lost his wealth. When he was affluent, his house was open to wayfarers and he gave much *tzeddakah*. After he lost his wealth, Zeide R' Motele secretly supported him so that he could continue his *chesed*.

The Czarist government set strict limitations on the travels of *tzaddikim*. Zeide R' Motele was not permitted to leave Hornosteipol. When he married off his son, R' Baruch Dovid, in Homel, he removed his traditional garb and dressed like a businessman in the hope that he would not be detected. However, due to the throng of *chassidim* who gathered for the wedding, the word got out that Zeide R' Motele was there, and he had to flee. Immediately after the *chuppah* he boarded a carriage to return to Hornosteipol.

En route, the driver suddenly stopped and said, "Rebbe, I am a highway robber. It is nothing for me to kill someone to rob him. I want you to give me a *berachah* for success. If you do not, I will kill you."

(Author's note: Is it not absurd, that a person who robs and murders has faith in the blessing of a *tzaddik*? Indeed, the Talmud acknowledges this phenomenon. "A thief who undermines a wall prays to G-d that he should not be detected" [*Ein Yaakov, Berachos* 63]. The Alter Rebbe explains this phenomenon. A person who is at so low a spiritual level is like someone in a dream. In a dream, gross contradictions can exist side by side. Although he is aware that there is a G-d, he can live with the absurd inconsistency of asking G-d's help in stealing.)

Zeide R' Motele did not lose his composure. "Listen to me," he said. "A similar incident occurred to my grandfather, R' Zusia, who was set upon by a group of thugs who threatened to kill him unless he gave them a *berachah*. My grandfather said, 'You will soon find the body of a *poritz*, who had a great deal of money with him. If you take that money and cease your evil ways, I give you my *berachah* for success. But if you continue in your ways, I assure you that you will be caught, and the police will lead you in chains before my house.'

"And so it was. Some of the group did *teshuvah* and were successful. Those who remained bandits were captured and led away in chains before R' Zusia's house.

"I have no wealthy *poritz* to give you, but I tell you this. If you will desist from your evil ways, things will go well for you. If you do not, I assure you, your end will be bitter. Mark my words! Now if you wish, you may kill me."

The driver sat stunned, then fell to Zeide R' Motele's feet, begged his forgiveness and asked him to guide him to *teshuvah*. He eventually became a *chassid* of Zeide R' Motele, and was known in Hornosteipol as "the *baal teshuvah* of Bobruisk."

Chapter 13
The Unidentical-Identical Coins

The *yichus* I described until now has not been confusing, but I will now change that.

As mentioned, Zeide R' Motele was a son-in-law of R' Chaim Halberstam (Divrei Chaim). The Zeide R' Motele's daughter, Sarah Miriam, married her uncle, R' Sholom Eliezer, a son of Divrei Chaim. Sarah Miriam's daughter, Chaya Fradel, married R' Benzion Halberstam of Bobov, my maternal grandfather. My father and mother were thus first cousins once removed.

R' Sholom Eliezer was rebbe in the Hungarian town of Ratzferd. Zeide R' Motele attended the marriages of his children, as did my maternal grandparents, the Bobover rebbe and rebbetzin.

Before they left Ratzferd, my grandfather asked Zeide R' Motele for a *shemirah* (a coin blessed as an amulet).

Halachah states that if a person has a *kamaya* (an amulet consisting of some writing on parchment) given by an acknowledged *tzaddik*, one may wear this on Shabbos, even though it is not an actual garment (*Orach Chaim* 301:25). A *shemirah* is another type of amulet.

That objects can have a potent effect is evident from the account in *II Kings* (4:29), where the prophet Elisha instructed his aide, Gechazi, to place his staff on the deceased child to resurrect him, and if Gechazi had not disobeyed the prophet's instructions, the staff would have performed the miracle (*Yalkut Shimoni, II Kings* 228:4).

At a funeral I attended in Israel, the cemetery attendant conversed with me. He said that he had no fear of the dead, despite the fact that he is constantly exposed to them.

"There was only one time that I was shocked," he said. "We were about to bury a man, when one of the family members said that he just recalled that the deceased had a coin, a *shemirah* given by R' Yisroel of Rhizin, which had been handed down to him. He had requested that this *shemirah* be buried with him. We waited until someone went back and brought the *shemirah*. When I put the *shemirah* into the hand of the deceased, he closed his hand tightly around the coin. That made me tremble."

When my grandfather asked Zeide R' Motele for a *shemirah*, my grandmother said she also wanted one. Zeide R' Motele took out two identical coins, and gave one to each.

In the process of packing, the two coins were placed in the same box, and my grandparents did not know which was whose. They returned to Zeide R' Motele, who asked them for both coins. He studied them for a moment, then said, "This one was yours, and this one was yours."

My Bobover grandfather said, "Zeide R' Motele did not dissimulate. He could easily have blessed a coin for each of us. His perception was such that he was able to discern which coin he had blessed for which grandchild."

My grandmother told me that when she was a child, she once said, "Believe me." Zeide R' Motele told her, "It is best not to use the expression 'Believe me.' It may be a form of a *shevuah* (sacred oath)." For the rest of her ninety-some years, she never again said, "Believe me."

Chapter 14
The Halachic Authority

At age eighteen, Zeide R' Motele wrote a classic work, *Chibur LeTaharah*, on the intricate laws of mikvah and *netilas yadayim* (hand-washing before eating). He quickly acquired eminence as a halachic authority, and complex halachic questions were addressed to him. He had correspondence with the leading halachic authorities of his time. His opinion was sought in cases of *agunah* (a woman whose husband has disappeared, but his death could not be confirmed). When granting a *heter* (permission to remarry) he always qualified that his decision was contingent on the concurrence of two more halachic authorities.

Zeide R' Motele used to say, "If I know that the husband is dead and I can find halachic support for this conclusion, I can give a *heter*. If I must rely on the halachah to tell me that he is dead, I cannot give a *heter*."

> A woman whose husband had been missing for several years came to Hornosteipol, bringing with her a *heter* authorized by two leading halachic scholars, but contingent on Zeide R' Motele's approval. Zeide R' Motele studied the *heter*, locked it in his desk drawer and said to the woman, "Go to Zhitomer."

The woman began crying. "I have been stranded and penniless without a husband for so long, and I wish to remarry. All I need is for the Rebbe to sign his name to the *heter* to release me from my bondage."

Zeide R' Motele repeated, "Go to Zhitomer."

The woman continued her tearful pleading, until the gabbai made her leave the room and said, "The Rebbe said to go to Zhitomer. Do as you were told."

No sooner did the woman alight from the train in Zhitomer than she recognized her husband in the train station. She created a furor, finally getting the police to bring her husband to the local rabbi, where he agreed to give her a *get*.

When word of this got around, the *chassidim* touted the event as an obvious miracle wrought by the rebbe. Zeide R' Motele shrugged it off. "It was the gabbai who made her go to Zhitomer," he said.

Zeide R' Motele said, "Had I signed the *heter*, the husband certainly would have died. Why kill a person without cause?"

Ruling on halachic questions requires more than book knowledge, as is illustrated by the following story.

One of Zeide R' Motele's *chassidim*, Baruch Yochanan's, on the afternoon of *Erev Pesach* (the eve of Passover), posed a *shailah* (halachic question) to Yankel the Rav. His wife had cooked the Passover food in a *chametzdig* pot. Yankel the Rav ruled that the food must be discarded.

Baruch Yochanan's asked Zeide R' Motele whether he could be at his *seder*, inasmuch as he had no food. Zeide R' Motele said, "Hurry home! If your wife has not yet discarded the food, you may eat it. It is kosher." Baruch Yochanan's happily discovered the food to be extant.

It eventually dawned on Yankel the Rav that Baruch Yochanan's would have no food for the festival. He asked his wife to send over whatever food she could spare, but the messenger returned with the food. Baruch Yochanan's said that the rebbe had ruled that the food was kosher.

Yankel the Rav was perplexed. How could the rebbe rule that food cooked in a *chametzdig* pot was kosher? He promptly went to Zeide R' Motele, who said, "Yankel, can you imagine that there is even a remote possibility that on *Erev Pesach* afternoon there could be a *chamitzdig* pot in Baruch Yochanan's kitchen? Don't you realize that his kitchen had been rendered completely *pesachdig* several days earlier?"

"But he told me that his wife had cooked the food in a *chametzdig* pot," Yankel the Rav protested.

Zeide R' Motele said, "Ay, Yankel, Yankel. It is not enough for a Rav to know the halachah. A Rav must also have *sechel* (good sense).

"Don't you know, women refer to the *pesachdig* pot used for boiling eggs as the *chametzdig pot*. (Perhaps this was because tiny fragments of straw are sometimes on the eggshell.) I didn't inquire, but you may ask and you will find this to be the case. *Sechel* would have told you that there could not be an actual *chamitzdig* pot in Boruch Yochanan's kitchen on the afternoon of *Erev Pesach*."

Zeide R' Motele corresponded in halachah with the leading Talmudists of his generation. The Beis Din of Jerusalem, under the presidency of the great gaon R' Yehoshua Leib Diskin, addressed a halachic question to him. He corresponded with R' Chaim Berlin, R' Eliezer of Telz, R' Yosef Shaul Nathanson of Lemberg, the *Beis Shlomo*, and of course, with his father-in-law, the *tzaddik* of Sanz. (In one responsa to a Hornosteipel *chassid*, R' Baruch Eisman of Kiev, R' Yosef Shaul writes, "Your letter arrived just as I was about to set out on a trip and I was extremely pressed for time. However, inasmuch as you were inquiring on behalf of R' Mordechai Dov, I am responding promptly.")

In the biography of R' Yoseph Kahanaman, *HaRav MiPonovezh*, it is recorded that the Ponovezher Rav especially favored Zeide R' Motele's halachic works, and often learned the response *Emek Shailah*, *Chibur LeTaharah* and *Turei Zahav*.

Zeide R' Motele compiled an authoritative work on the complex issues involved in writing a *get* (Jewish divorce). This manuscript was lost in the fire that destroyed his library. After this loss, Zeide R' Motele refused to rule on any problem involving a *get*.

Turei Zahav, sefer by Zeide Reb Motele

Chapter 15
The "Yosha Kalb" Episode

Although Zeide R' Motele was only peripherally involved, I am recording this fascinating episode as I had heard it from my father, because I believe it is the least distorted version available.

My great-great-grandfather, R' Yehoshua of Kaminke (the Kaminke Zeide), had a daughter, Yentele, who married Moshe Chaim, a fine young Torah scholar. Moshe Chaim was the son of R' Tzemach, a highly esteemed *chassid*. It was later discovered that R' Tzemach had dabbled in "applied Kabbalah." The Kaminke Zeide said that had he known this in advance, he would not have approved of the marriage.

"Applied Kabbalah" is an esoteric subject, whose use is sharply discouraged. A person with knowledge of applied Kabbalah is said to have access to unusual powers. The sages teach that by use of applied Kabbalah, some of the sages created a human robot. The legend of the Golem of Prague, in which R' Yehudah Loewi of Prague (MaHaral) is said to have created a human robot, is well-known. Unless one is extraordinarily spiritual and thoroughly knowledgeable in applied Kabbalah, one risks becoming subject to demonic forces.

Not too long after the marriage, Moshe Chaim suddenly disappeared, without leaving a clue as to his possible whereabouts. Yentele was left an *agunah*, and could not remarry because she had no *get* (halachic divorce) from her husband.

After several years, Moshe Chaim suddenly reappeared. Where had he been? He would not say. Why had he left? He would not say. He had undergone some rather dramatic changes in appearance, being wild-eyed with a straggly beard that so covered most of his face that it appeared to be growing out of his eyelashes. Yentele, however, recognized him, and his identity was confirmed beyond doubt when he related to her personal information that only her husband could have known.

Abruptly, when people spoke to him, he appeared not to recognize them. When they called him "Moshe Chaim," he said he could not understand why they are calling him by that name, because he was Yosha Kalb. He said he lived in another city (Krasna, if I remember correctly), and that he had no idea who this Moshe Chaim was.

When the people of Krasna were contacted, they confirmed that there was indeed a Yosha Kalb in their community who had recently disappeared. They identified this man as the Yosha Kalb they knew. He had a wife in Krasna, who identified him as her husband, Yosha Kalb, and again he related private information to her which only her husband could have known.

(Author's comment: Up to this point, the story is somewhat dramatic but not yet exotic. While dual or multiple personalities are uncommon in psychiatry, there have been such cases. This is known as a "dissociative neurosis." A person switches identities, not by malingering, but by sincerely believing that whatever identity he has at the moment is his only one. Person "A" may abruptly become Person "B," and he has no awareness of anything he did as Person "A." These are intriguing cases. In forty-five years of psychiatric practice I encountered only one such case. Books have been written about this unusual and dramatic phenomenon. But what follows distinguishes this case from the typical dissociative reaction.)

Investigation revealed that on the very same day that Moshe Chaim married Yentele in Kaminke, Yosha Kalb married his wife in Krasna, whose distance from Kaminke was such that no one could have been in both places at the same day. Extensive research left no doubt to the accuracy of the dates. This person appeared to have been in two distant places at the same time!

The Kaminke Zeide swore that this was Moshe Chaim, and the rabbi of Krasna swore that this was Yosha Kalb!

When he was in his Moshe Chaim identity, he was prevailed upon to give a *get*. But then the question arose, given that there is testimony that this man was Yosha Kalb and could not possibly have been in Kaminke on the day Yentele was married, could there be absolute certainty that he was Yentele's husband and that he could release her from the marriage with a *get*?

The halachic question was brought to Zeide R' Motele, who wrote an opinion validating the *get*. He sent a personal message to Yentele, that although he had ruled halachically that the *get* was valid, to "do me a personal favor and not remarry," and blessed her with longevity. Indeed, Yentele lived to a ripe old age, and never did remarry. My mother remembered Aunt Yentele well.

One of Zeide R' Motele's sons, R' Baruch Dovid, arranged his responsa for publication. One time Zeide R' Motele sent him on an errand. When he returned, he realized that the manuscript had been tampered with. The responsum on the Moshe Chaim-Yentele *get* had been removed.

Eventually, the Yosha Kalb identity disappeared. If anyone dared address Moshe Chaim as Yosha Kalb, he became violent.

Moshe Chaim lived in Cracow, supporting himself by begging. When my parents lived in Cracow, he would come regularly for a handout. My mother would run and hide when he came in. "He looked more like a jungle beast than a human being," she said. But my father would hold him by the lapels and demand, "Tell me the truth! Who are you?" He always managed to wrestle himself loose.

And so ends this strange story. *Chassidim* assumed that R' Tzemach's dabbling in applied Kabbalah had resulted in demonic interference, and that the dual personality was some type of demon who could indeed be in two distant places at the same time.

Chapter 16
Torah Teachings of His Forebears

The writings of Zeide R' Motele's forebears are voluminous. I am presenting only a fragmentary sampling of the teachings that influenced him.

If you feel a desire to do something, divest yourself from all gratifications and advantages that it may bring, because then you can
Baal Shem Tov easily be objective and see all the pros and cons, clarify the best way to do it, or perhaps not do it at all. Remember this rule, because it is of great use.

A person who thinks himself to be a great scholar, a *tzaddik* of many good deeds and fear of G-d, and thinks that because of his superior status he is above associating with anyone else but humbles himself because it is a mitzvah to be humble, can be compared to a person riding in a coach who falls asleep. While he sleeps, the driver takes the coach up the slope of a tall mountain, then continues on level land. When this person awakens and sees he is on level land, he thinks that he was always traveling on level land, having no idea that they had ascended a tall mountain. When does he bcome aware of this? Only when they begin traveling down the other side of the mountain.

A person may think himself to be "on the top of a mountain," with feelings of *gaavah* (vanity). He may have no idea that he is spending his entire life in *gaavah*. He discovers this only when he suddenly finds himself heading downward.

A true *tzaddik*, one who is free of all blemish, does not see anything bad in other people; therefore he has true *ahavas Yisrael* (love for other Jews). One who has not yet corrected all his own defects may find fault in others, but he should know that he is in fact faulting himself. This is contained in the verse: "Deliver me from all my transgressions" (*Psalms* 39:9), i.e., forgive all my sins. How shall I know that I have been forgiven? When You will arrange it that I see no faults in degenerates, then I shall know that I have been cleansed of sin.

Where does the Torah tell us that one must consult a *tzaddik* for guidance, and that learning *mussar* from books is not sufficient? The Torah says, "G-d said to Moses, 'Write this as a remembrance in the Book and recite it in the ears of Joshua' " (*Exodus* 17:14). Why was G-d's instruction to Moses to write it in the Book not enough? Because this notwithstanding, He said, "recite it in the ears of Joshua." Speak to him face-to-face. The most effective thing is to hear the message from a *tzaddik*.

The Talmud says (*Kesubos* 67b), " One who *squanders* (for *tzeddakah*) should not squander more than one-fifth." The term "squanders" indicates that the person thinks he is wasting his money. In other words, he has no joy in giving, but rather feels that he is depriving himself. He is essentially giving against his will. For this person the sages set a limit of one-fifth. But if one gives *tzeddakah* joyously and takes pleasure in giving because he believes that G-d will replenish him, he may give as much as he wishes, and there is no set limit to his giving.

(The Baal Shem Tov could not tolerate the preachers who sharply rebuked their audiences.) "Those whom G-d loves, He chastises" (*Proverbs* 3:12). His chastisement is out of His intense love. But those who chastise because they feel they are better than others or because they wish to be compensated for their preaching may bring down harsh judgments on Israel.

It is written: "The chastening of G-d, my son, you should not despise" (*Proverbs* 3:11). This can also be read (by moving the comma) as, "You may preach the chastening of G-d, but be careful not to despise my sons, the children of Israel, to be critical of them."

The most certain way to provide for the *neshamah* is by doing three things: (1) to recite *Tehillim (Psalms)* with a fiery passion; (2) to do kindnesses for others, not only by giving *tzeddakah* but by personal involvement and effort; and (3) to love other Jews to the point of self-sacrifice.

King David says, "I greatly rejoice in Your words, like one who has found great spoil" (*Psalms* 119:162). However the verse in 19:11 says,

The Baal Shem Tov's Parables "They (the words of G-d) are to be desired more than gold and fine gold," which means that they are *more* precious than spoils. Furthermore, why the emphasis on finding *great* spoil?

But the meaning can be understood by a parable. Suppose a person comes across a huge treasure, and he cannot possibly take the whole treasure in one trip. He carries away only that which he can and fears that before he returns for more, someone else might come and take away the rest. Even though he is happy with what he has taken, his joy may be shrouded by his frustration that there is so much more that he cannot take now.

That is the attitude toward learning Torah to which King David refers. Although one rejoices over what one learns, he is frustrated by the awareness that there is so much more that he does not know. Indeed, the more one learns of Torah, the more one is aware of its infinity which one cannot grasp.

The Baal Shem Tov defined true love of G-d with a parable.

A wise king wished to test which of his ministers truly loved him. He had a palace constructed with many walls serving as barriers to the throne room where he resided. In each wall there was a door, and in front of each door he put piles of gold and silver coins.

He then invited his ministers. Each one, upon encountering the piles of gold and silver, filled his pockets and gleefully went home. One minister, who truly loved the king, ignored the gold and silver and made his way through all the doors, because he was driven by the desire to see the king himself. His love for the king exceeded his love of gold and silver.

The Baal Shem Tov taught that rather than simply banish any improper desires one may have, it is better to transform and convert them by directing them toward proper goals. He gave this parable:

A proprieter of a store detected a thief trying to break in. He began shouting to summon the neighbors for help. Hearing the cries, the thief ran away.

Sometime later, the thief tried to break into another store. This proprieter remained quiet, and sneaking up stealthily, threw a rope around the thief and bound his hands and feet. Only then did he call the neighbors to help him take the thief to prison.

The *yetzer hara* is like a thief, who wishes to rob people of their good traits and lead them to wrongdoings. There are two ways to cope with it. (1) You can drive it away, but this will allow it to return at a later date; or (2) subdue it, bind it hand and foot, and convert it toward proper goals. There is then no way it can return for another attempt to do damage.

When Mashiach comes (speedily in our time), there will be constant unity and perfection. This unity is the secret of the construct of the stature of Mashiach. The Baal Shem Tov said that every single Jew must prepare and rectify that portion of the structure of Mashiach that pertains to his *neshamah*.

R' Nochum of Czernoble

As is known, "Adam" is the mnemonic for "Adam, David, Mashiach." The stature of Adam was from one end of the world to the other; i.e., it included the *neshamos* of all Israel. After Adam sinned, his structure lessened. However, Mashiach will rectify his sin and there will be a complete structure of all the *neshamos* of Israel, as it was before Adam's sin. Therefore, every single Jew must prepare his portion of Mashiach (*Meor Eynaim, Pinchas*).

"These are the offsping of Noah—Noah was a righteous man, perfect in his generations" (*Genesis* 6:9). Rashi comments that some of our sages interpret the phrase "in his generations" in praise of Noah, that he was a *tzaddik* even in a wicked generation, and had he lived in a generation of *tzaddikim* he would have been an even greater *tzaddik*. Others give a critical interpretation: Noah was a *tzaddik* relative to the wicked people in his generation. Had he been in the generation of Abraham he would not, by comparison, have been considered a *tzaddik* at all.

R' Nochum asks, if one has the option to give a favorable interpretation, why give an unfavorable one? Furthermore, inasmuch as the Torah refers to him as "perfect," how can one say that in the generation of Abraham he would have been imperfect? Perfection is not a relative concept.

R' Nochum cites the Talmudic statement that every person has a potential portion in *Gan Eden* (Paradise). If a person is a *rasha* (sinful), he forfeits that share, which is thereupon given to a *tzaddik* (*Chaggigah* 15a). R' Nochum states that this also true in this world. There is some good in every person. If a *tzaddik* reprimands a *rasha*, and the latter rejects the reprimand, the portion of good within him attaches to the *tzaddik*.

The Baal Shem Tov said that the words that go from the mouth of a *tzaddik* to the ear of the listener are of a spiritual nature. Hearing is also of a spiritual nature. If his words are rejected by the *rasha*, they revert back to him along with the *rasha's* spiritual capacity to listen. This increases the spirituality of the *tzaddik*.

The apparent critical interpretation of "in his generations" given by the sages is not at all unfavorable. Rather, it explains how Noah came to be a perfect *tzaddik*. It was because his generation rejected his reprimand, and his spirituality increased by virtue of his receiving their spiritual listening capacity which they forfeited (*Meor Eynaim, Noah*).

In narrating the episode of Amalek's attack on the Israelites, the Torah says, "It happened that when Moses raised his hand, Israel was stronger, and when he lowered his hand, Amalek was stronger" (*Exodus* 17:11). The Talmud asks, was the battle contingent on the position of Moses' hands? It answers that when the Israelites looked upward and prayed to G-d, they triumphed. When they were lacking in prayer, i.e., looking downward and depending on their own prowess, Amalek grew stronger (*Rosh Hashanah* 29a). R' Nochum remarked that this does not satisfy the Talmud's question. It was not the position of Moses' hands that made the difference, but the attitude of the Israelites.

R' Nochum answered that the service of G-d is contingent upon one's *daas* (understanding), because it is in his depth of understanding of the infinity of G-d, that He encompasses the universe and that He permeates the universe, that brings one to *yiras Hashem* (awe of G-

d) and *ahavas Hashem* (love of G-d). The Zohar states that *zero'os olam* (*Deuteronomy* 33:27) can be taken literally as "the arms of the world, that the right arm represents *ahavah* and the left arm represents *yirah*" (*Tekunei Zohar* 17a).

The Zohar states that Moses was the *daas* of Israel (*Zohar, Pekudei* 221a). It was Moses who gave Israel *daas* of G-d. It was his mission to fulfill "and you should *know* (*daas*) that I am G-d (*Exodus* 1:7, 10:2, 16:12). The Talmud means that when the Israelites had greater *yiras Hashem* and *ahavas Hashem*, i.e., "they uplifted the arms of Moses" and were victorious. When they were lax in these two ways of serving G-d, Amalek grew stronger. It was their degree of devotion to G-d that is represented by the positions of Moses' hand (*Meor Eynaim, Beshalach*).

"You shall love your G-d with all your heart," (*Deuteronomy* 5:5). The Talmud comments, "with all your heart" means with both the *yetzer tov* (good inclination) and the *yetzer hara* (evil inclination) (*Berachos* 54a). How are we to understand loving G-d with the *yetzer hara*?

We may ask, how can it be expected of a person to love G-d? How can one love a Being that he cannot see or have any concept of whatsoever? The answer is that we believe that everything in existence has its source in G-d. Hence, if we feel an affection or desire for anything physical, we should reflect, Where did this object have its origin? If we realize that its origin is in G-d, and that it is only a tiny fragment and faint shadow of its Source, then how much more is the Source desirable and deserving of our love.

However, the *yetzer hara* may so blind a person that he does not go beyond his immediate sense experiences and does not reflect upon the Source of the object of his desire. Therefore, the Talmud, referring to the *yetzer hara*, says, "If this vulgar being confronts you, take him to the house of Torah study" (*Kiddushin* 30b). The temptations of the *yetzer hara* are all for transient pleasures, and then one is left with nothing. The Talmud quotes G-d as saying, "I did create the *yetzer hara*, but I created Torah as its antidote" (ibid.). Study of Torah can enable one to wrest free of the *yetzer hara's* grasp.

This is what is meant by *teshuva me'ahavah, teshuva* out of love. We can use the love for physical objects as a stimulus to love of the Source of all pleasures, which is G-d (*Meor Eynaim, Vo'eschanan*).

The Talmud says that if two people sit together and do not discuss Torah, that place is a place of the scornful, and in support of this,

R' Zusia of Anipoli cites the verse in *Psalms* (1:1) (that the virtuous person) never sat where the scornful sit (*Ethics of the Fathers* 3:3).

R' Zusia asked, "How does the verse in *Psalms* prove that if two people sit together and do not discuss Torah, it is a place of the scorners?" He explains that a person's actions create an atmosphere that may persist after the person leaves. Thus, if a person studies Torah or does a mitzvah, he creates an atmosphere of *kedushah* (sanctity) which rests on that place. On the other hand, if one commits a sin, that leaves a trace of *tumah* (impurity) at that place.

The Mishnah wonders, why would two people not join in discussion of Torah? It concludes that it must be because the place where they are sitting must have been a place where scornful people had gathered, and the trace of *tumah* that remained discouraged them from discussing Torah. This is what the verse in *Psalms* means. A virtuous person seeks places of *kedushah*, and avoids places where scornful people may have assembled. Places like that are not conducive to Torah observance (*Menoras Zahav, Vayigash*).

The *yetzer hara* is very cunning. Although humility is a most virtuous trait, the *yetzer hara* may crush someone and make him think himself to be so worthless that he feels his acts are of no consequence. He may think, "Who am I to stand in prayer before G-d? Why should I deny myself worldly pleasures? I can never achieve any spirituality." This is a spurious humility. We can read this into the words of the Psalmist, "*Ki Hillel rasha al taavas nafsho*" (10:3). A *rasha* can make himself humble as Hillel, but it is a false humility, serving only to gratify his heart's desire.

At times like this a person should think, "I am a descendant of the Patriarchs. I am a beloved child of G-d with a Divine *neshamah*. I am too good to do things that are beneath my dignity (*Menoras Zahav, Beshalach*).

The Torah says, "Distant yourself from a false word" (*Exodus* 23:7). This verse can also be read to mean, "From a false word, you become distant." Speaking a false word causes you to become distant from G-d (*Menoras Zahav, Mishpatim*).

The Talmud says, "Jews are holy. There is a person who wants to give *tzeddakah* but has nothing to give, and there is a person who has what to give but does not want to" (*Chullin* 7b). The obvious question is, Why is a person who has the means to give but does want to give called "holy?" Tosafos states that this refers someone who does not want to give, but gives against his will because he is embarrassed to refuse. He, too, is considered holy.

R' Zusia said that he could not understand Tosafos' explanation. Why would someone who gives *tzeddakah* grudgingly be considered holy? He wept unceasingly because he was unable to understand Tosafos.

That night the author of Tosafos appeared to him in a dream and said, "Do not cry. I will tell you what I meant. The Mishnah says that when a person does a mitzvah, he creates an angel (*Ethics of the Fathers* 4:13). An angel has a spiritual body, comprised of fire and air, as the Psalmist says, 'He makes winds His messengers, flaming fires His ministers' (*Psalms* 104:4). The angel also has a *neshamah*. The physical performance of a mitzvah creates the angel's body, and the *kavannah* (intent) of the mitzvah creates its *neshamah*.

"The person who wants to give but has nothing to give has only the good intent, which creates only the *neshamah* of the angel, but not its body. The person who gives grudgingly has performed the physical act, which creates the body of the angel, but because he does not have good intent, it is a body without a *neshamah*. Because all Jews have a mutual reponsibility to do mitzvos, the physical act of the one person and the good intent of the other person are joined in creating a complete angel. The two together, therefore, are holy."

(As was noted earlier, R' Shneur Zalman said that R' Zusia is a "true gaon," because he gleans his knowledge from the source.)

... If a person downgrades the role of the body, and rejoices primarily in the joy of the *neshamah*, this is a simple and easy way to the

R' Shneur Zalman (author of *Tanya*)

fulfillment of the mitzvah, "Love your neighbor as yourself" toward every Jew, from the greatest to the least. If one spurns the physical cravings of the body and focuses on the *neshamah*, whose greatness and value with its Source being the Living G-d is inestimable, then we are all united (in our *neshamos*) as having one Father. This is why all Jews are factually brothers in that the source of all their *neshamos* is the One G-d. It is just that their bodies are separate. Therefore, those who give primacy to the body and give the *neshamah* a secondary status cannot have true love and brotherliness. (Their love) can only be dependent on something. This is why the sage Hillel said that fulfillment of this mitzvah (Love your neighbor as yourself) contains the entire Torah, and that all else is commentary. Because the foundation and root of Torah is to elevate the *neshamah* far, far above the body, to the origin and root of all the worlds, and to bring down the light of the Infinite One to the congregation of Israel... That is, to be united in the Source of all *neshamos* to be one, and not, heaven forbid, for there to be any separation of *neshamos*...(*Tanya*, chap. 32).

There is a greater intellect and a lesser intellect. The lesser intellect reacts, and can become angry at anything which is in any way contrary to his own will. That is not so with the greater intellect, which can tolerate in his mind things that are contrary to his will, and because of his superior wisdom, is not angered at all (*Likutei Torah, Shir HaShirim*).

We can see that if the intensity of an affect was only commensurate with the capacity of the intellect, then the extent of the affect could never exceed the reach of the intellect. If so, why do we sometimes see a very intense affect of the heart, whose corresponding source cannot be found in the intellect? How can the offspring exceed its progenitor? We must, therefore, conclude that the initial origin of affects is not only in the intellect, because then they could not exceed it...The first source of the formation of an affect is above the intellect, and it only traverses the intellect. That is why the reaction of an affect can be greater than the capacity of the intellect (*Siddur, Shaar HaTefillin*).

... With the acts of mitzvos which a person does he draws down upon himself the actual light of the Infinite One...This is why mitzvos are compared to a candle: Just as when one lights a candle the house becomes full of light and brightness, so to with the performance of mitzvos, a brightness is drawn to all the worlds...

... Drawing the G-dly light from concealment to revelation is through the performance of mitzvos. It is just as with planting, where most seeds are not edible. A seed is only a tasteless nucleus, but when it is planted in the earth and receives the energy to grow it produces edible fruit, although the seed itself was inedible ... So also with the performance of mitzvos that are clothed in physical objects, like *tefillin* on parchment and *tztizis* of wool, and so with other mitzvos, when a Jew wears them (*tefillin*) on his head, it is in the category of Divine revelation (*Torah Ohr, Shemos*).

… I shall disclose to you my meager opinion about taking on fasts or wanderings. I do not believe that G-d desires this, and this is not what I was taught by my holy teachers. The advisable thing is to pray with boundless *simchah* (joy) which will disperse all improper thoughts. Even if these should occur, they will fall away like the chaff before the wind.

As is it is written, "Israel rejoices in its Creator" (*Psalms* 149:2). *Simchah* is to take extreme pleasure in the greatness of the Creator, in the praise mentioned in the *siddur*, as if one would actually see the glory of a mortal king, which is revealed in the splendor of his throne, which brings joy to those who run toward him to see him. This is how one should feel in prayer…(Letter to R' Levi Yitzchok of Berditchev).

Prayer can transform even physical desires to the Divine will…Just as when silver which is thoroughly admixed with dross and is put into the flame of a refining furnace, the parts are separated off so that the fine silver emerges. The longer the silver is in the flame, the more it is drawn from its concealment (in the admixture) until the minutest traces of dross are eliminated. So it is with the fiery passion of prayer; all the impurities are separated off and even the minutest traces do not remain… (*Likutei Torah, Bamidbar*).

R' Ahron of Karlin

There is a difference between dejection and broken-heartedness. Dejection is nothing but a disappointment that one's needs have not been satisfied. It is selfish feeling, the frustration of one's desires.

One should not be concerned with the deprivation of one's desires. Rather, one should be concerned whether G-d's desires are being met.

If I could exchange places with the Patriarch Abraham, I would not do so. True, I would have the pleasure of being the great Patriarch, but what would G-d gain thereby? There would still be only one Abraham and one Ahron. That would be simply selfish.

Broken-heartedness is the feeling that one has been derelict in the performance of one's duties. The awareness that one has not done enough can motivate a person to action.

A person who is dejected will withdraw and mope, perhaps lie in bed all day. He cannot tolerate the presence of other people and cannot tolerate himself. He seeks an escape from the world. By contrast, a person who is broken-hearted will seek to study Torah and do mitzvos to correct his shortcomings.

But there is a fine line between broken-heartedness and dejection. One must be careful that broken-heartedness not result in dejection (*Giborei HaChassidus*).

R' Mordechai of Czernoble (Czernoble Maggid)

The Talmud says, "One should not arise to pray other than with a serene attitude" (*Berachos* 30b). Yet, it says: "He was filled with exuberant self-assurance as he went in the paths of G-d (II *Chronicles* 17:6)." How can we reconcile an attitude of exuberance with profound serenity?

Everything is dependent on the condition of one's mind. If one's thoughts are focused on reverence of G-d all day, it is easy for him to pray with intense devotion, undisturbed by intrusive thoughts. However, if a person allows his mind to digress from concentration on G-d, then he may find many alien thoughts intruding during prayer. Therefore, this person must meditate with profound serenity prior to prayer, and pledge himself to *teshuvah*; i.e., that he will make an effort to keep his mind focused on reverence for G-d throughout the day. He will then be able to pray with exuberance, with an appreciation of the supremacy of G-d (*Lekutei Torah, Ki Sisa*).

"You have wrapped yourself in a cloud that no prayer can pierce" *Lamentations* 3:44). Chassidic masters often gave favorable interpretations to ominous verses. This verse in *Lamentations* states that in His wrath, G-d refused to hear the prayers of Israel.

R' Mordechai said that the Hebrew words lend themselves to another and very different interpretation. In *Exodus* (19:9) it says that G-d said to Moses, "Behold! I come you in the thickness of a cloud." If a person feels himself to be in the thickness of a cloud that is a barrier between him and G-d, and is heart-broken because he feels that he cannot reach G-d, this feeling of humility is so meritorious that his prayers can rise high. It is only when a person is vain that his prayers may be feeble (*Lekutei Torah, Succos*).

"The Children of Israel did everything that G-d commanded Moses, so did they do" (*Numbers* 1:54). The phrase "so did they do" appears redundant.

R' Mordechai explained that in every mitzvah there are many esoteric meanings (*kavannos*) which are an integral part of the mitzvah. However, relatively few people know all these meanings.

If a person is totally and sincerely devoted to doing the will of G-d, then even if he is not able to think of all the esoteric intricacies, G-d considers his sincere devotion as if he indeed had performed the mitzvah with all its *kavannos*.

This is what the Torah is saying. Moses certainly knew all the esoteric *kavannos* which G-d had revealed to him, but most of the Israelites did not. However, because they were sincere in wanting to do the mitzvah in its entirety, just as G-d had given it to Moses, G-d considered it as though they had indeed done so. "The Children of Israel did everything that G-d commanded Moses, so did they do." Their performance of the mitzvos was equivalent to Moses' (*Lekutei Torah, Bamidbar*).

There is indeed a form of devotion that comes easily, but it is the polar opposite of the G-dly inspiration. We can see that many people have an

R' Dov Ber (Mittler Rebbe)

external manifestation (of devotion) with their imaginary ideas during prayer, which come out as superficial cries from a heart of flesh, with no internal light or spirit, and are not really at all to G-d. In this kind of meditation there is no internalization…

Two people may hear a G-dly subject. One has a sense of hearing that causes him to be influenced by the essence of the subject, of the truth in the subject, and he understands its profundity. The other is not impressed by the essence of the subject, but rather by the way it is explained, and in the fine manner in which it was presented. The first one has a much greater sensitivity, and inasmuch as he grasps the essence of the subject, he is no longer in need of explanations...

Moses said to G-d, "When I come to the Children of Israel and say to them, 'The G-d of your forefathers has sent me to you,' and they say to me, 'What is His Name?'— what shall I say to them?"

G-d said to Moses, "I Shall Be As I Shall Be." And He said, "So you shall say to the Children of Israel, 'I Shall Be has sent me to you' " (*Exodus* 3:13-14).

R' Dov Ber pointed out that Moses did not say, "They will *ask* me what is His Name," but rather "They will *say* to me what His Name is."

G-d's response was that the Hebrew word for "I Shall Be" is *eheye*, whose letters have the numerical value of twenty-one. This Name the Israelites may know. But to you I say, "I Shall Be As I Shall Be" (*eheye asher eheye*) which is twenty-one times twenty-one, or four hundred forty one, which is the numerical value of *emes* (truth). The Israelites may indeed have an inkling of G-d, but only you, Moses, know the truth of G-d.

If a person looks about at all the happenings that surround him, he can see the Providence of G-d as He conducts everything in the world. In this way, business people may have an advantage over those who are full-time Torah scholars, because they have the opportunity to see the hand of G-d in everything that transpires in the world.

The Talmud says, "A person should always incite his *yetzer tov* over the *yetzer hara*. If he does not succeed in this, let him learn Torah. If he is

R' Yaakov Yisrael of Cherkassy (Cherkassy Zeide)

still not successful, let him recite the *Shema*. If he is still unsuccessful, let him remember that one day he will die (and will have to give an accounting of his life and deeds before the Heavenly Tribunal)" (*Berachos* 5a).

"*If he dos not succeed*, let him learn Torah." How can he even begin to battle the *yetzer hara* without Torah? It must be that inherent within every Jew there is an aversion to evil which just needs to be activated…There is a nucleus within every Jew that does not wish to be separated from its source in G-d for even a moment. This is why a Jew has the capacity to choose martyrdom if forced to renounce his faith in G-d (ibid. *Tazria.* compare Tanya, chapter 18, (*Emek Tefillah, Mikeitz*)).

A person should pray with love of G-d and in awe of G-d, and this is not attainable unless one meditates prior to prayer on who he is, what he was created for, before Whom is he speaking, and that the ability to speak was instilled in him by G-d. One must meditate on *teshuvah* before prayer (ibid. *Beshalach*).

The way one can tell if he prayed properly is whether he feels there has been a change in him, that he is different now than before he prayed. Is he more distant from physical cravings than he was before he prayed? For if the passion for improper desires and traits is present after prayer, this indicates that his feelings of devotion to G-d during prayer were an illusion. The fiery passion of true prayer consumes and eliminates the passion for earthly objects (ibid. *Vayigash*).

The Torah states that Jacob said, "If G-d will be with me, will guard me on this way that I am going…and G-d will be a G-d to me," (*Genesis* 28:21). On the latter part of this verse, Rashi comments, "That there will not be any deviation among my children." But how could Jacob ask this of G-d? Whether a person remains loyal to G-d or not is a matter of *bechirah* (free choice), and G-d does not determine whether a person will do good or evil.

In the *Amidah* we pray, "Bring us back to Your Torah," and the Psalmist prays, "Lead me in the way of eternity" (*Psalms* 139:24). These prayers, too, seem to be in conflict with *bechirah*.

The essence of true faith is that one believes that G-d provides all one's strength and ability to do anything, both physically and spritually, and that without His help, one could not do anything. Whereas it is true that G-d has given a person *bechirah*, a person may *return this bechirah* to G-d, saying, "I have absolute faith and trust in You to do everything for me."

(Author's note: I have given this example elsewhere: Two children each receive a gift of money. One runs off to the candy and toy stores and spends his money of his own free will. He is likely to have a stomachache from indulging in candy, and within several days, his toys may be broken. The other child gives the money to his father, saying, "Invest it for me in what you think is best." Both exercised their *bechirah*. The first child did so foolishly. The second child did not lose his *bechirah*. Rather, he used it wisely to let his father decide for him.

I believe this is what the Cherkassy Zeide is referring to. G-d indeed gives us *bechirah*. If we have true *emunah* (faith and trust), we return our *bechirah* to him.)

Chapter 17
Zeide R' Motele's
Torah Discourses

eide R' Motele's halachic works were edited personally by
him. His Torah discourses on Chassidus were tran-
scribed by *chassidim* who had heard them. I prefaced
these excerpts with some of those of his forebears, which
enables us to see how he blended their chassidic insights into his
own unique thought.

The Torah ends with וּלְכֹל הַיָּד הַחֲזָקָה וּלְכֹל הַמּוֹרָא הַגָּדוֹל אֲשֶׁר עָשָׂה
מֹשֶׁה לְעֵינֵי כָּל-יִשְׂרָאֵל "By all the strong hand and awesome power that
Moses performed before the eyes of all Israel," the final letter being ל.
The Torah begins with בְּרֵאשִׁית, the first letter of which is ב. Inasmuch
as the Torah is continuous, without beginning or end, its last letter
and first letter together form the word לֵב (heart). How does this en-
hance our service of G-d?

The Torah writings state that in the Egyptian captivity, *daas* (knowledge and understanding) was in exile: The Israelites lacked the
knowledge that G-d is the Creator Who brought and maintains everything in existence. That is why G-d said that by His delivering them
from Egypt, "You will *know* that I am G-d" (*Exodus* 6:7). The manifest

miracles of the exodus was so that they should *know* and recognize that G-d is the Creator Who rules and directs everything in the world, as Moses said, "You have been *shown*, in order to *know* that Hashem is G-d" (*Deuteronomy* 4:35). Therefore, the deliverer was Moses, who represents the *daas* of Israel, to bring *daas* to the Israelites.

In this final exile that we are in, it is primarily the *middos* (character traits) that are in exile. The *daas* (knowledge and understanding) we have does not filter down to the *middos*. Even if one has an intellectual understanding that G-d is the Creator and that He observes everything, this has not impacted upon the *middos*. One can be attracted to physical desires because one is disconnected from one's *daas*.

This can be corrected if one gives some thought before doing any action, to just what it is that he is doing and why is he doing it. This is what is meant in *Proverbs* (24:6), "With strategy you can do battle." It requires strategy to channel desires toward proper goals and not follow them unthinkingly as animals do.

The Torah refers to intellect and knowledge as "vision, or the eyes of the mind" ergo, "You have been *shown* (made to see), in order to *know*." *Middos*, on the other hand, have their origin in the heart, which is the source of all desires. (Even colloquially we say, "I desire it with all my heart" or "my heartfelt gratitude [author].)

That is the connection between the end of the Torah and the beginning. "That Moses performed before the eyes of all Israel," that he endowed them with the "eyes of the mind" to *know* that there is a G-d (ending with ל), connecting with the ב of בראשית, forming the word לֵב, to indicate that the intellectual knowledge must affect the *middos*.

The Torah continues בָּרָא is related to the word בריאות (health), and Elokim is the numerical equivalent of הטבא (nature). This means that the intellect can channel the *middos* so that one has a healthy approach to nature, and can avoid falling prey to the *yetzer hara's* seduction of following one's natural inclinations as do lower forms of life. The Torah then continues, "the heaven and the earth," to indicate that with the intellectual guidance of the desires of the heart one can achieve the *tikkun* (rectification) of everything, both spiritual and mundane (*Peleh Yoetz, Bereishis*).

"A window shall you make for the ark...put the entrance to the ark in its side (*Genesis* 6:16) ... And to Shem, also to him were born; he was the ancestor of all those who lived on the other side; the brother of Japheth the elder" (ibid. 10:21).

What purpose is there in the detailed description of Shem?

We must understand this as a teaching in the service of G-d.

In the *Shema* we say to "love your G-d, with all your heart, with all your soul and with all your resources." The Talmud says that "with all your heart" means with both the *yetzer tov* and the *yetzer hara*, "with all your soul" means even to sacrifice your life, and the word for "your resources, מְאֹדֶךָ, is related to the word מדה, meaning "measure;" i.e., for whatever measure G-d gives you, you should be grateful (*Berachos* 54a).

The sages are referring to three levels of *ahavah* (love). "With all your heart" refers to the hidden nucleus of love for G-d that is present in every Jew, which was bequeathed to us by the Patriarchs. In prayer, one should arouse this hidden love and bring it into the open. This is accomplished by suppressing the physical desires that obscure it, and this is what is meant "with both the *yetzer tov* and the *yetzer hara*;" in other words, with *all* your heart.

"With all your soul" refers to an intense love for G-d, that one's soul so pangs for a closeness to Him that one would willingly surrender one's life. This is the level of the *baal-teshuvah*, whose awareness of the sins he committed cause him to be so incensed with the bodily desires that led him to sin, that he would willingly dispose of his physical body.

"With whatever measure G-d gives you, be thankful to Him" is the highest level of *ahavah*. At this level one takes pleasure in his closeness to G-d at all times and in all places. This fulfills the Divine desire to have a presence in the earthly world.

"These are the generation of Noah, Noah..."(*Genesis* 6:9). The word נח means "pleasant," and the repetition of נח refers to both a supernal pleasantness and a pleasantness on earth. This is achieved with the third level of *ahavah*, which must, of course, be preceded by the first two levels.

The words אִישׁ צַדִּיק equal the numerical value of תפלה (prayer), indicating the achievement of the first level of *ahavah*, revealing the hidden nucleus of *ahavah* through prayer.

"He was perfect in his generations and walked with G-d" (ibid.) refers to the second level of *ahavah*. The Talmud says that a person should realize that with one *mitzvah* he can tip the balance of his entire generation toward a favorable judgment, and that one sin can tip the balance of his entire generation to a harsh judgment. The awareness of the gravity of one's sins can make one reject his physical drives, to the point of even yielding one's life.

Having achieved the first two levels of *ahavah*, one can then reach the level of "Noah walked with G-d," the level of taking pleasure in everything G-d does to one.

"*Shem*" refers to prayer, as is evident from the verse in *II Samuel* 8:13. The phrase "And to Shem, also to him were born" means that prayer should give birth, i.e., to bring out the hidden nucleus of *ahavah* (the first level). One can then ascend to the second level, "he was the ancestor of all those who lived on the other side" by realizing the far reaching consequences of one's sin which can bring a harsh judgment upon one's entire generation.

The highest level of *ahavah* is then attainable. "The brother of Japheth" refers to beauty, יופי, which is the beauty of the constant state of pleasure one has in being close to G-d under all circumstances.

"A window shall you make for the ark." The word for ark, תֵּבָה, also means "word," and the teaching is to bring light into each word of prayer. And "put the entrance to the ark (תבה=word) in its side" means to provide, through prayer, a portal for the Divine presence to be in this earthly world (*Peleh Yoetz, Noah*).

"Jethro, the minister of Midian, the father-in-law of Moses, heard everything that G-d did to Moses and to Israel, His people, that G-d had taken Israel out of Egypt" (*Exodus* 18:1). Rashi states that Jethro came because he heard about the miracle of the dividing of the Reed Sea and the battle of Amalek. Why does Rashi cite these two incidents, when the Torah says that Jethro heard "everything that G-d did to Moses and Israel?"

This is a teaching for the service of G-d. There are two things that can upset one's service of G-d. The first is of an earthly nature, which

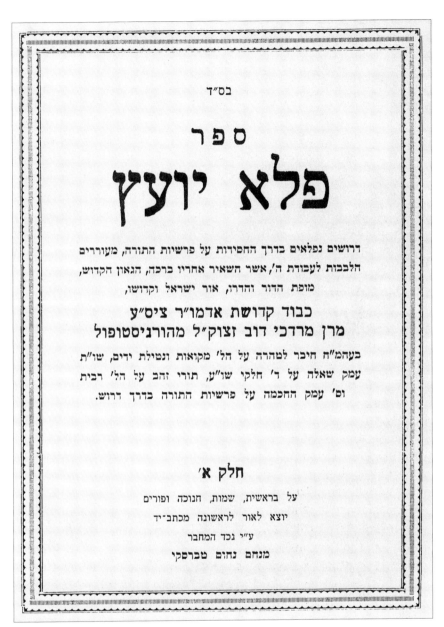

בס"ד

ס פ ר

פלא יועץ

דרושים נפלאים בדרך החסידות על פרשיות התורה, מעוררים
הלבבות לעבודת ה', אשר השאיר אחריו ברכה, הגאון הקדוש,
מופת הדור והדרו, אור ישראל וקדושו,

כבוד קדושת אדמו"ר ציס"ע
מרן מרדכי דוב זצוק"ל מהורניסטופול

בעהמח"ח חיבר לטהרה על הל' מקואות ונטילת ידים, שו"ת
עמק שאלה על ד' חלקי שו"ע, תורי זהב על הל' רבית
וס' עמק החכמה על פרשיות התורה בדרך דרוש.

חלק א'

על בראשית, שמות, חנוכה ופורים

יוצא לאור לראשונה מכתב-יד

ע"י נכד המחבר

מנחם נחום טברסקי

Peleh Yoetz, "Chassidic Discourses of Zeide R' Motele"

is the concern that a person has about earning his livelihood. This can
be a bottomless pit, because one always seeks to earn more for fear
that one will not have enough. But the Psalmist says, "There is no

lack for those who revere Him" (*Psalms* 34:10). If one has true reverence of G-d and knows that He is the Creator that conducts everything in the world, he would not exhaust himself in endless pursuit of greater earnings. The Talmud says, "I have never seen an animal or bird that had to work at a craft to earn their sustenance. Inasmuch as other forms of life were created to serve man, why must I exert myself to earn a livelihood? It is only because by my doing wrong deeds I have forfeited the sustenance that G-d provided for me" (*Kiddushin* 82a). This is indicated in the battle of Amalek who attacked "when you were faint and exhausted" (*Exodus* 23:18). This is the work of the *yetzer hara*, to cause you to exert and spend yourself in the pursuit of excesses.

One can also be upset for spiritual reasons, namely that one has not achieved feelings of love for and reverence of G-d, and this causes one to become dejected. However, a person should always rejoice that he has been privileged to serve G-d. This is what the Talmud means that a person should be happy with his portion (*Ethics of the Fathers* 4:1), in the portion of G-dliness that is in everyone's *neshamah*.

At the crossing of the Reed Sea the Israelites reached the understanding of rejoicing in their privilege to serve G-d, as they declared, "This is my G-d and I will build Him a Sanctuary," that each person, according to one's abilities, will make a dwelling place for G-d.

The word Jethro, יתרו in Hebrew, refers to excesses. One can avoid the pursuit of excesses, both physical and spiritual, if one will bear in mind "everything that G-d did to Moses and Israel," that G-d provides for everyone. Trust in G-d will eliminate exhaustive exertion: "There is no lack for those who revere Him." In the spiritual realm, one will not be disillusioned and disheartened if one has not achieved his aspirations, and will be able to serve G-d in joy.

Rashi, therefore, explains that the triumph over Amalek, who attacked "when you were faint and exhausted," is the triumph over the exhaustion one brings upon oneself in pursuit of excesses, and the dividing of the Reed Sea, where Israel achieved serving G-d with joy (*Peleh Yoetz, Jethro*).

Zeide R' Motele's gabbai, R' Dan, complained that he felt crushed because he could not muster the proper *kavannah* for prayer. In a letter to R' Dan, Zeide R Motele writes:

> "Let me explain the verse, 'I will proclaim the praise of G-d with my life, and I will sing to G-d as long as I exist' (Psalms 146:2). True, a person should put his entire life into his prayer and be willing to surrender his life to G-d in every word of prayer. That is 'I will proclaim the praise of G-d with my life.' But one must also be able to pray joyously even if one does not have that level of kavannah, and feels no more than that he just exists. That is 'I will sing to G-d as long as I exist.'
>
> "Should it happen that one feels very lowly, he should take heart that even someone as slight as I am can approach the King of Kings and speak to Him directly."
>
> Zeide R' Motele continues, "Remember the Talmudic tale of Elijah pointing out two people who he said would merit Gan Eden because they went around cheering up people who were morose.
>
> "A person should always be in simchah. It is the work of the yetzer hara to make one dejected. We have a constant struggle with the yetzer hara, and as in any battle between two opponents, sometimes one gains the upper hand, sometimes the other. But you should never give up the battle to vanquish the yetzer hara's effort to depress you."

In addition to chassidic discourses, Zeide R' Motele wrote brilliant essays on Torah, following in the footseps of Torah commentaries who showed that many of the episodes related in the Torah were in concurrence with halachic principles developed centuries later. These essays are gathered in *Emek Chochmah*.

Chapter 18
A *Tzaddik* Departs from This World

In the year 5658 (1898), Zeide R' Motele related that his uncle, R' Dovid of Talna, appeared to him in a dream and said, "In heaven they desire to bring up two 'Moteles.' I interceded on your behalf to extend your life five years because the world has need of you."

Zeide R' Motele's children became very anxious because of this dream, and their fears intensified when shortly thereafter, their uncle R' Motele of Selichov died.

In spite of deteriorating health, Zeide R' Motele's devotion to Torah and service of G-d continued unabated, as if with superhuman strength.

In 5663 (1903), the children approached Zeide R' Motele and said that they wished to publish his writings. He responded, "You are quite right. Your grandfather, the *tzaddik* of Sanz, published his works in the last year of his life."

On the Shabbos night of *Selichos*, Zeide R' Motele wrote a responsa (*Emek Shailah, Orach Chaim* 7). Upon completion, he gave it to his son, R' Baruch Dovid, to review, while he continued to receive his *chassidim* who had come to him for guidance before Rosh Hashanah and Yom Kippur. After the *melave malka* (Shabbos night meal in honor of the departing Sabbath Queen), he reread the responsa. He erased the date which read, "Eve of the first day of the week" (which was the customary way he wrote a date at night), and instead wrote, *motzaei Shabbos* (the close of Shabbos). Clearly, he knew that he would not live through the ensuing week. He, therefore, dated the responsa *motzaei Shabbos*, since his relationship was with the week that had just passed.

On Sunday night, Zeide R' Motele then retired to his room to rest, and when Babba Raitza heard a deep groan, she rushed into the room to find Zeide R' Motele breathing his last. On the twenty-second day of Elul, 5663, the heavens rejoiced in greeting the second "Motele" for whom they had waited the past five years.

Chapter 19
Zeide R' Leibele

Although Zeide R' Leibele was the third of Zeide R' Motele's four sons, the *chassidim* chose him as the successor to his illustrious father. Zeide R' Motele used to refer to Zeide R' Leibele as "my *chacham*" (wise person). In a letter to his *chassidim*, Zeide R' Motele had written about him as "his words are as my words and his hand is like my hand," which testified to his qualifications as their spiritual leader.

Zeide R' Leibele followed in his father's footsteps. Virtually all his income was alloted for *tzeddakah*. When he was asked why his own children are less deserving than the recipients of his *tzeddakah*, he replied "There will be people who will look after their needs, but if I do not look after the poor to whom I give, no one else will."

Zeide R' Leibele used to deliver Torah discourses and relate accounts of the great *chassidim*. Although he never chastised in his discourses, *chassidim* felt his words penetrated into their hearts, and often shed tears of *teshuvah*. Many of his discourses were recorded, but were lost when he fled from the Communist persecution.

Zeide R' Leibele's humility was profound. He used to comment on the verse, "An altar of earth shall you make for Me" (*Exodus* 20:21), upon which Rashi comments, "It must be made for Me from its very begin-

R' Benzion Yehudah Leib Twerski
(Zeide R' Leibele)

ning." Zeide R' Lebele said that "an altar of earth" represents humility. In *Shir HaYichud* we read, 'I will build an altar with my broken heart." Earth also represents humility, as we find in the words of the Patriarch Abraham, "I am but dust and ash" (*Genesis* 18:27). All other mitzvos do not necessarily have to be initiated with the highest degree of *lishma* (pure motivation) and may even be done for ulterior motives, as the Talmud says, "A person should always do mitzvos, even if not *lishma*, because this will eventually lead him to doing them *lishma*" (*Pesachim* 50b). But the altar of earth, which represents humility, must *begin* with *lishma*, with absolute sincerity and the purest of motivation, because humility that is with ulterior motives is actually the polar opposite, *vanity*.

His guidance was according to his teaching that a person should always conduct himself in a straightforward manner. He remarked on the verse: "With scheming shall you do battle" (*Proverbs* 20:18), that if you deviate from the straight path, it will result in struggle.

Zeide R' Leibele's life was fraught with distress. As the president of the regional funding project (Kollel Vohylin) for the Torah community in Eretz Yisrael, he sent money to Eretz Yisrael, which was then under Turkish rule. Inasmuch as Russia and Turkey were in hostilities, he was accused of treason, and he narrowly escaped imprisonment. Following the Communist revolution, he cared for the hundreds of Jews who had fled their villages. When the cold and hunger resulted in a typhus epidemic, there were few who dared to bury the dead for fear of contagion. Zeide R' Leibele's son, R' Moshe Meshulum Zusia was one of the few who sacrificed his life to bring Jews to burial, and he died in the epidemic.

That Zeide R' Leibele's perceptions were above the normal is evident from the following story.

In Russia it was customary that during the week, soup was served following the meat, whereas on Shabbos, the soup was served first. One Friday night, Zeide R' Leibele's *chassidim* were at his table, when the soup was served. Zeide R' Leibele said, "What reason could there be for changing the order of the dishes on Shabbos? We should have the meat served first like always."

The soup was taken back, and when the chicken was served, they noticed a broken thigh bone that had grown together, which made the chicken and hence the soup *treife*. Zeide R' Leibele was thus spared from accidentally eating *treife*.

The following Friday night they asked him in what order to serve the dishes, and he said, "Why, it is customary to serve the soup first, isn't it?"

The *chassidim* said that Zeide R' Leibele obviously had *ruach hakodesh* (Divine inspiration) which protected him from eating *treife*. Zeide R' Leibele said, "What kind of *ruach hakodesh?* We all know that nothing happens unless it is so decreed from above, and this applies also to thoughts that occur to a person. It had never previously occurred to me to question why the order of dishes is different on Shabbos. When this question came to mind last week, I realized that there must be a reason behind it. That you call *ruach hakodesh?*"

When Zeide R' Leibele prayed, he was totally detached from any earthly contact. I recall that when he said the *Amidah,* he would sway from side to side with his eyes wide open, since it is customary to keep the eyes closed unless one is looking into a *siddur*. My late brother, R' Shloime asked him, "Why does Zeide keep his eyes open during the *Amidah.*" Zeide R' Leibele answered, "Really? My eyes were open? I didn't know."

When we were sitting *shivah* after my father's death, one of the visitors was David Schaffner, a Chicago businessman whom I knew well from his periodic visits to Milwaukee. (My father told me that when he was born, the midwife in charge of the delivery was David's grandmother, who was 102 and blind.) David related the following story:

David had worked up his business as a distributor of tobacco products, and received an offer to sell his business for $160,000. In the 1920's this was a huge sum, which David considered a windfall. At that time, Zeide R' Leibele was visiting Chicago, and David's wife insisted that he ask the rebbe for a *berachah*. Zeide R' Leibele inquired what his business was, and David related that he was going to sell his business for $160,000, which he would then be able to invest. Zeide R' Leibele told him not to sell it, because that would not be to his advantage. However, David did sell the business, with a non-competition clause for three years. In the crash of 1929, David's investments were wiped out and he was penniless.

When Zeide R" Leibele subsequently visited the United States, David's wife again insisted that he see the rebbe for a *berachah*. David told him about his misfortune, and Zeide R' Leibele did not chastise him for not having followed his advice. Instead, he asked him whether he had any remaining properties. David said that he had a piece of land for which he paid $600, but which was now worth only $200. Zeide R' Leibele gave him a coin as a *shemirah* and said, "With G-d's help that property can bring you a million dollars." David said, "I left the rebbe with the impression that he does not have the faintest grasp of economics. How can this next to worthless property net me a million dollars?"

A short while later David received a call from a city official, offeirng him $10,000 for the property. David said he must consult with his attorney, who told him that if the city needs this land they will pay more. David sold the property to the city for $15,000.

The three years of the non-competition clause had passed, and with the $15,000 David went back into the tobacco business. A friend of his, whom David had helped in the past, had married into a wealthy family that owned the rights to the midwest tobacco trade. Inasmuch as David was back in the tobacco business, this friend offered him an exclusive distributorship. That year, David made one million dollars.

David said, "I lost my initial wealth because I did not listen to the rebbe. It was the rebbe's *berachah* that turned my near-worthless property into $15,000, which enabled me to go back into business and eventually acquire the distributorship. I made the million dollars that the rebbe promised me."

A man in Chicago came to Zeide R' Leibele for a *berachah* for his wife, who had entered the ninth month. Zeide R' Leibele said, "What? Your wife already went to have the child? It should be with *mazal*."

Inasmuch as Zeide R' Leibele was hard of hearing, the man thought he had not been understood, so he repeated his request for a *berachah*, because his wife was in the ninth month. Again, Zeide R' Leibele said, "What? Your wife already went to have the child? It should be with *mazal*." When this happened for the third time, the man gave up and went home, only to find that his wife had already gone to the hospital.

In 1920, he fled from Communist persecution to Cracow, and in 1925 moved to Antwerp. In 1934 he moved to Israel and settled in Tel Aviv. He returned to Antwerp to sell his home and settle permanently in Israel. The outbreak of World War II made his return to Israel impossible. He managed to leave Belgium shortly before the Nazi occupation, and settled in Chicago.

When I attended yeshivah in Chicago, I lived with Zeide R' Leibele. Every other week I would go home to Milwaukee for Shabbos. One time, as I bid farewell to Zeide before leaving for Milwaukee, he said, "I was just going to mail this letter to your father. Take it with you." He then opened his desk drawer, took out a postage stamp and tore it up. When he saw my surprise, he said, "You are not a postman. I do not have the right to deny the postal service their fee."

His many sufferings took their toll, and he suffered a disabling stroke. I was with him during his last years, and at his bedside on the Friday night that he died.

He was in a coma the last few days of his life, and, sitting at his bedside, I suddenly heard him mumbling words. I set my ear close to his lips, and heard the words of the angelic hymn, "The power and the trustworthiness are to Him Who lives forever." With the last verse, "The adoration and grace are to Him Who lives forever," he returned his *neshamah* to G-d. It was the 28th day of Teves, 5761 (1950).

The Author's Genealogy

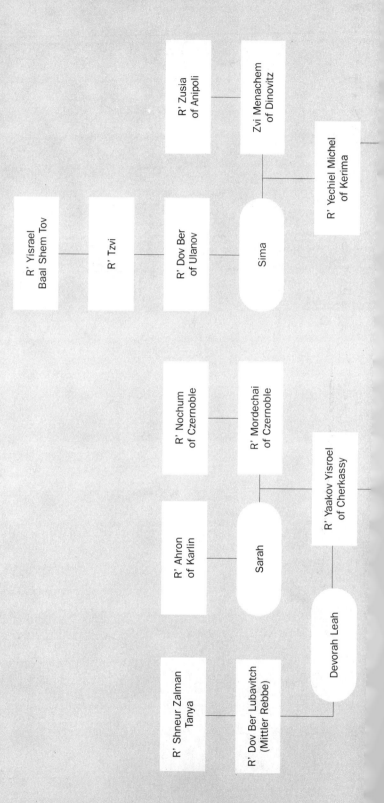

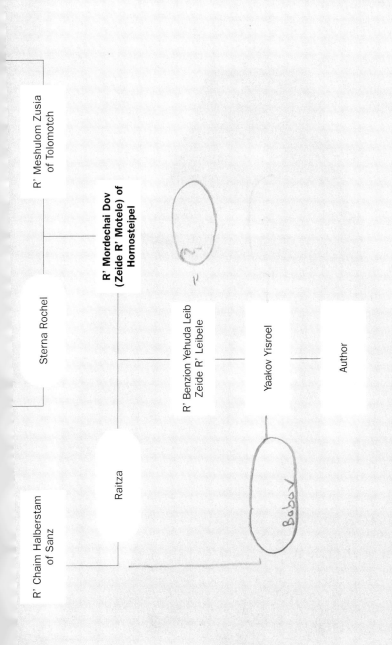

R' Chaim Halberstam
of Sanz

Sterna Rochel

R' Meshulom Zusia
of Tolomotch

R' Mordechai Dov
(Zeide R' Motele) of
Hornosteipel

Raitza

R' Benzion Yehuda Leib
Zeide R' Leibele

Yaakov Yisroel

Author

Baba

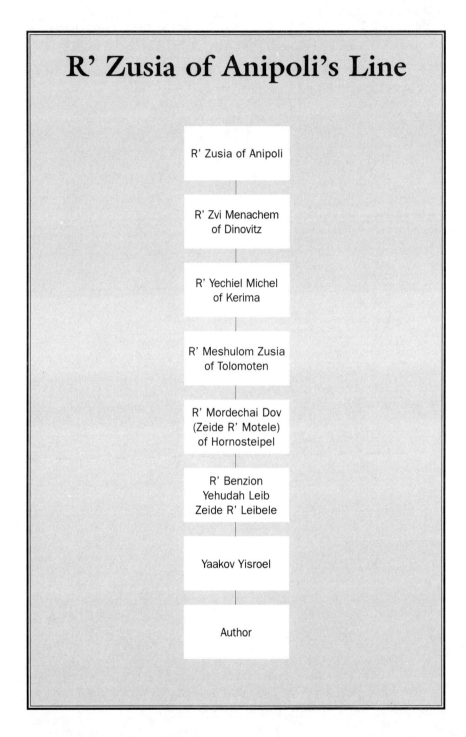

R' Zusia of Anipoli's Line

R' Zusia of Anipoli

R' Zvi Menachem
of Dinovitz

R' Yechiel Michel
of Kerima

R' Meshulom Zusia
of Tolomoten

R' Mordechai Dov
(Zeide R' Motele)
of Hornosteipel

R' Benzion
Yehudah Leib
Zeide R' Leibele

Yaakov Yisroel

Author

Baal Shem Tov's Line

R' Yisroel Ben
Eliezer
Baal Shem Tov

R' Zvi

R' Dov Ber of
Ulanov

Sima

R' Yechiel Michel
of Kerima

R' Meshulom
Zusia
of Tolomoten

R' Mordechai Dov
(Zeide R' Motele)
of Hornosteipel

R' Benzion
Yehudah Leib
Zeide R' Leibele

Yaakov Yisroel

Author

Czernoble Line

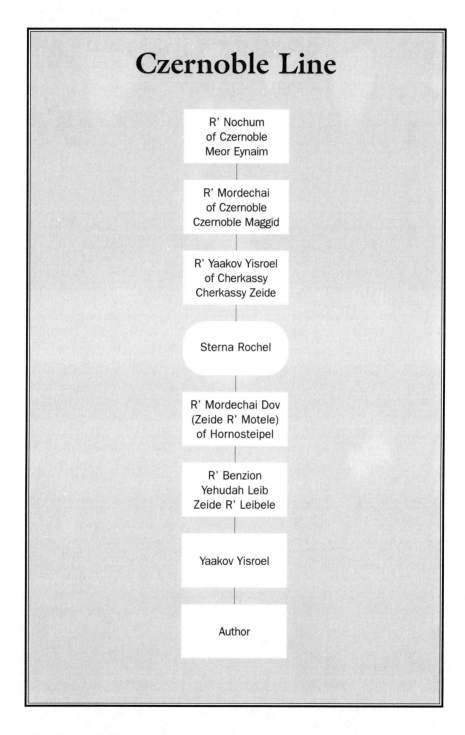

R' Nochum
of Czernoble
Meor Eynaim

R' Mordechai
of Czernoble
Czernoble Maggid

R' Yaakov Yisroel
of Cherkassy
Cherkassy Zeide

Sterna Rochel

R' Mordechai Dov
(Zeide R' Motele)
of Hornosteipel

R' Benzion
Yehudah Leib
Zeide R' Leibele

Yaakov Yisroel

Author

Chabad Line

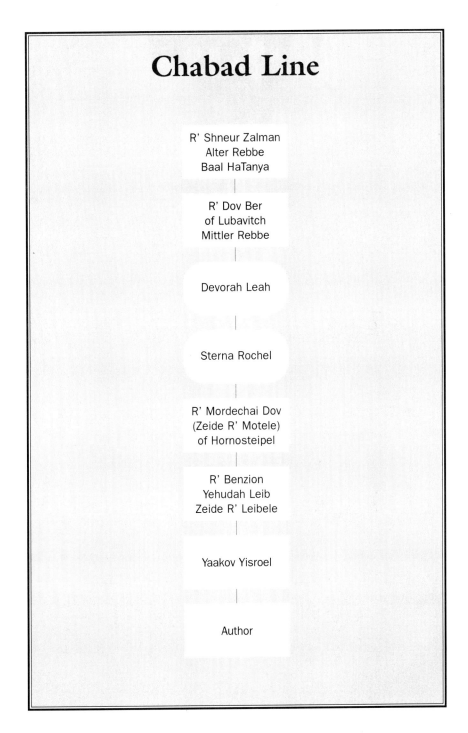

R' Shneur Zalman
Alter Rebbe
Baal HaTanya

R' Dov Ber
of Lubavitch
Mittler Rebbe

Devorah Leah

Sterna Rochel

R' Mordechai Dov
(Zeide R' Motele)
of Hornosteipel

R' Benzion
Yehudah Leib
Zeide R' Leibele

Yaakov Yisroel

Author

Karlin Line

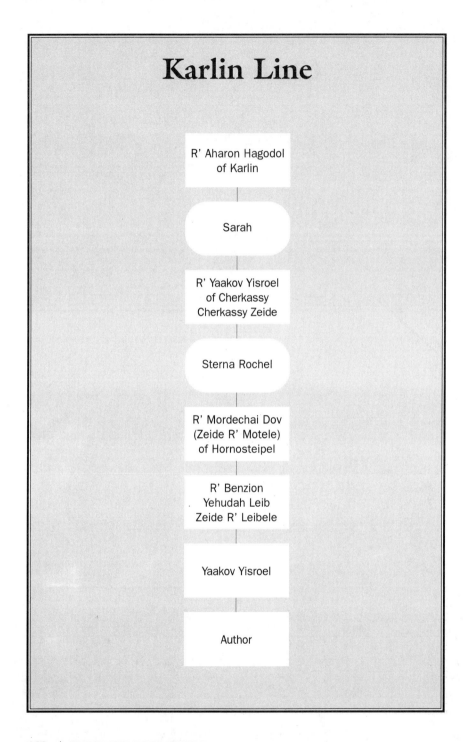

R' Aharon Hagodol
of Karlin

Sarah

R' Yaakov Yisroel
of Cherkassy
Cherkassy Zeide

Sterna Rochel

R' Mordechai Dov
(Zeide R' Motele)
of Hornosteipel

R' Benzion
Yehudah Leib
Zeide R' Leibele

Yaakov Yisroel

Author

Sanz and Baruch Taam Line

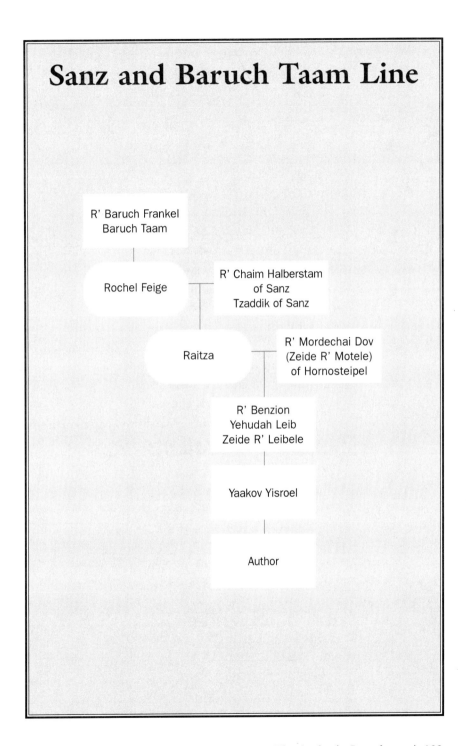

R' Baruch Frankel
Baruch Taam

Rochel Feige

R' Chaim Halberstam
of Sanz
Tzaddik of Sanz

Raitza

R' Mordechai Dov
(Zeide R' Motele)
of Hornosteipel

R' Benzion
Yehudah Leib
Zeide R' Leibele

Yaakov Yisroel

Author

This volume is part of
THE ARTSCROLL SERIES®
an ongoing project of
translations, commentaries and expositions
on Scripture, Mishnah, Talmud, Halachah,
liturgy, history, the classic Rabbinic writings,
biographies and thought.

For a brochure of current publications
visit your local Hebrew bookseller
or contact the publisher:

Mesorah Publications, ltd

4401 Second Avenue
Brooklyn, New York 11232
(718) 921-9000
www.artscroll.com